Teen Spirituality

WITH
EMOTIONAL
CORE
THERAPY

Robert A. Moylan

CONTENTS

DISCLAIMER

This book details the author's personal experiences with and opinions about mental health and relationships. The author and publisher are providing this book and its contents on an "as is" basis and make no representations or warranties of any kind with respect to this book or its contents. The author and publisher disclaim all such representations and warranties of merchantability and healthcare for a particular purpose. In addition, the author and publisher do not represent or warrant that the information accessible via this book is accurate, complete, or current.

The statements made in this book are not intended to diagnose, treat, cure, or prevent any specific condition or illness. Please consult with your own physician or mental healthcare provider regarding the suggestions and recommendations made in this book.

Neither the author nor the publisher will be liable for any damages arising out of, or in connection with the use of this book. This is a comprehensive limitation of liability that applies to damages of any kind, including (without limitation): compensatory, direct, indirect, or consequential damages; loss of data, income or profit, loss of or damage to property and claims of third parties.

You understand that this book is not intended as a substitute for consultation with a licensed healthcare practitioner, such as your physician or therapist. Before you begin any healthcare program or change your lifestyle in any way, you will consult with your physician or healthcare provider to ensure that you are in good health and that the examples used in this book will not harm you.

This book provides content related to mental health and relationships. As such, your use of this book implies your acceptance of this disclaimer.

Teen Spirituality

WITH
EMOTIONAL
CORE
THERAPY

*A Simple and Effective Method
to Empower the Mind*

BY ROBERT A. MOYLAN

ACKNOWLEDGEMENTS

I would like to thank my daughter, Anna, who brings me great joy. Also, a special thanks to my editor, Mike Valentino. His patience and expertise were invaluable during the writing of this book. I would also like to give special thanks to Dr. Jack Johns, Duane, George, and many other friends for all of their help and support.

AUTHOR'S NOTE

The goal of this book is to reach anyone who desires to learn how to live a full life of vitality and energy. To live life to its fullest, without any regrets. One of the best ways to do this is to get the most out of each day you live. One of the best ways to get the most out of each day you live is to not let feelings of fear, anger, and grief inhibit or cripple your lifestyle. For people of faith, this includes prayer and a connectivity with God or spirituality. Emotional Core Therapy can help people with that important facet of their life. It is the simplest and most effective behavioral psychology treatment available worldwide for most relationship stress including addictions, depression, anxiety, anger, personality disorders, childhood emotional trauma, sports psychology, and marital therapy. ECT is not a religiously based approach, and will work even if you do not adhere to any faith tradition. However, for people whose religion is a crucial aspect of their lives, ECT will be a perfectly natural fit. It never asks you to do or say anything that would be contrary to your beliefs. In fact, it will help strengthen your beliefs as it lifts up your spirits and allows you to clear the clutter from your mind, therefore seeing both the physical and spiritual dimensions of your life as if through new eyes. Yes, it may even lead you to a spiritual renewal and awakening that you had never before thought possible.

How does one test the validity of a psychology or self-help book? What you have to do is list the top ten to twenty stressful events in your life. With the 8 step ECT Flowchart in my book you can process almost any relationship stress that occurs in life. It is really quite that simple. All you have to do is reflect on the ten to twenty most stressful events in your life. Then write those events down on a sheet of paper. Once you have read Emotional Core Therapy (the process sinks in through repetition best) you can then process your ten stressful events through the ECT Flowchart. You will then have verified evidence that ECT is the only behavioral psychology approach that is so simple you can use it for almost any relationship stress in your life. No other psychology approach, religious teaching, or educational process can claim these results.

Up till now, the vast majority of counselors, social workers, psychologists, psychiatrists, and ministers have been relying on psychology techniques/approaches such as Rational Emotive Therapy/ REBT, Cognitive Behavioral Therapy/ CBT, Dialectical Behavioral Therapy/ DBT, Acceptance and Commitment Therapy, Psychoanalysis, Motivational Interviewing, 12 Steps, even religious teachings such as Buddhism and Christianity to heal people. In this book, we will offer approaches to ECT that come from Christian, Muslim, Buddhist, Jewish, Hindu, Taoist, and secular perspectives. At the core of each of these belief systems is the quest for inner peace and tranquility, which is why these practices blend so smoothly with ECT, which at its core is designed to help each individual learn to quiet their mind.

ECT uses many of the same techniques as some of the other aforementioned psychological approaches listed above. However, ECT also includes my own unique research and findings and condensed the ECT process to eight steps. With ECT, there is renewed hope that addictions and mental health issues can be treated more effectively throughout the world.

I realize, however, that you may be asking, can we measure a psychology approach like we do a major league pitcher throwing a fastball, or an Olympic runner racing in a 100-yard dash? Unfortunately, we cannot measure any psychology approach, including ECT, over an extended period of time. When I say extended period of time I mean three to six months or longer. Why? Too many variables exist that would adversely affect an accurate measurement. For example, the training of mental health professionals can widely vary, as can people's educational and aptitude levels, resources, environments, etc. Not to mention we all experience stress differently.

That's why, as mentioned earlier, the only effective way to truly measure any psychology approach is with direct scientific evidence. This means the process has to work every time. To help you understand ECT, try and list ten to twenty stressful events that you face in your daily life. Then try and process them through whatever psychology approach, religious teaching, or educational approach that you currently use. Then do the same with my eight step ECT Flowchart. There will be your evidence. Only ECT effectively treats the root cause of human relationship stress. How does ECT do this? There exists a cause and effect relationship with stress. The ECT Flowchart depicts how the natural state of stress occurs. For every relationship stress a person encounters on a daily basis, one thing happens with certainty every time. What is that? One of the four true feelings, joy, grief, fear, or relief will arise and occur. These four temporary feelings cause stress to humans by altering one's central nervous system. This reality is at the heart of ECT's unmatched success!

You can't deny, suppress, or ignore the four true and authentic feelings for very long without hurting yourself in some fashion. The four true feelings will happen no matter what you do on a daily basis whether at home, school or at work. Illegal drugs and alcohol can only alter, dull, or dampen, your five senses and four feelings. That's why emotionally healthy people realize that taking drugs or medications won't really change the conditions you face in life. Only your perception changes. Altering your mind and yourself with depressants and stimulants will only delay your emotional growth. Why? The four true feelings are with us hourly and daily our whole lives.

The good news is that ECT is the simplest and most effective psychology approach to treat nearly all psychological disorders and relationship stress that you will ever face in your life. The only exceptions would be cases where permanent physical or psychological damage has occurred. Even simple everyday activities such as throwing out your back lifting a heavy object or changing your tennis swing can be understood clearer using the ECT Flowchart.

I've never encountered a stressful human interaction that I wasn't able to comprehend how I feel using the eight step ECT Flowchart. On some rare occasions it is hard to distinguish the exact variable that caused you stress. For example, hitting a golf shot out of a deep rough on a downhill slope on a cold windy day. You mishit the shot badly. Often, the variables are too many to accurately know what caused you stress. What you can always recognize is the true and authentic feeling of grief or fear that follows taking the poor shot. This is similar to a college fraternity boy who has a hangover from drinking vodka, beer, smoking marijuana, and staying up late. He is not exactly sure what caused the pain – but he sure knows he feels the pain/ grief.

Every stressful event in a person's life (for example, breaking up with a boyfriend/ girlfriend, failing a class, arguments with parents, messing up a play and losing the game for your team, etc.) can all be traced back to the four feelings. Why not honor and learn from these four feelings? Why run away from them or disconnect from them? That is the focus of ECT! When you learn from emotions you become more aware of what limitations your body and mind has regarding the four emotions.

If you are a religious person, ECT will become a part of your prayer life, meditation and spiritual devotional time. We will see in this book practical examples of how adherents of Christianity, Islam, Buddhism, Judaism, Taoism and Hinduism as well as secular people all can use ECT to enrich and fulfill their everyday lives.

Think of it this way. Two gold diggers are on a sandy beach hunting for precious metals. One miner has a metal detector that detects hundreds of metals, many of them useless. The other miner has a metal detector that only detects the four true minerals of value (for example, gold, silver, platinum, and aluminum). Who has the simpler and more effective method of mining? Obviously the second gold digger is more efficient. The same goes with emotions. We will show in the book there are hundreds of names for emotions. When you can reduce the number down to the four true emotions, you will have a much easier job learning from them. Why? The four true and authentic emotions serve as a navigation tool or compass in life by helping you choose healthy relationships that bring you joy and leaving unhealthy relationships that bring you grief and fear. All my clients that complete therapy successfully have real power and confidence in their lives. Why? They leave therapy knowing they can have a relaxed, meditative state of being, very close to what is termed "mindfulness" in psychology circles. Then when any type of stress occurs in their lives they have the full confidence in the eight step ECT Flowchart. They know that they can identify, process, and release this situational stress and get back to a normal relaxed state of being. No other psychological, religious, or educational approach can do this as they are continually redirecting you away from your true emotional state.

Another example I use is a school teacher in a playground who has to supervise 150 children. Another teacher has to supervise four children. Who has the easier job? Obviously the school teacher who supervises four children has the less stressful job. We breakdown needs in our ECT Flowchart down to four categories also. The needs and demands people face from their relationships are what cause stress. So when we simplify the needs and emotions for people we can help them learn more quickly and effectively, regardless of age.

Stress, in the form of the four true feelings comes hourly and daily for people. The key point for all healthy individuals is to learn to cathartically release these emotions. Perhaps you are thinking, aren't prayer and meditation supposed to do that? Prayer and meditation are indeed important for religious people, and ECT is not designed to replace these virtuous practices. Instead, ECT works right alongside these spiritual pursuits like a perfect match. ECT is the most inclusive psychology approach worldwide as it can incorporate any psychological technique that is proven to help release emotions. I give over 20 examples in my books on how to successfully release emotions. Even common ways of relaxing such as yoga, Pilates, sitting in a warm Jacuzzi, listening to music on headphones, etc., can be easily incorporated into the eight step ECT Flowchart.

ECT is now being used throughout many parts of the world. Since joining Linkedin last year, I have now been endorsed by thousands of professionals throughout the world. ECT was the top rated book in two categories (Emotions and Mental Health) on Amazon in 2014. Approximately ten thousand people have read and reviewed ECT without any major criticisms of the ECT process. Why? It works as a process to identify and release stress if used correctly. This has included people from many various faith traditions, along with those who practice no particular religion. In fact, part of the beauty of ECT is that it can work for anyone, regardless of your upbringing, beliefs or spiritual disposition.

Currently, I teach ECT to medical and mental health professionals both online and in person for continuing education units (CEUS) for their license renewal. This includes psychologists, social workers, counselors, nurses, marriage and family therapists, physical therapists, chiropractors, massage therapists, and several other professions. ECT is approved by a dozen United States licensing boards for continuing education credit and renewal.

I have a strong commitment to better the world and make it a more peaceful place. The psychology field can unite us as human beings if we work together and educate teens and adults on learning to really love themselves and love others. My hope is to have all religious organizations and mental health providers utilize ECT and bring people throughout the world closer together as human beings.

Lastly, remember that knowledge is power! You and your loved ones all have been hurt and in pain from emotional stress of some kind from a relationship. It is only human nature to be a bit "stressed out" from time to time, and sometimes these situations seem even tougher for teenagers. With ECT you will now have the tools to help yourself and to cleanse your soul daily for all of your life.

This book teaches a simple step by step approach that brings you closer to mastering the mind. The ECT Flowchart that you see on the adjacent page will be placed throughout the book at the end of each chapter. This will be beneficial for those visual learners who want to monitor their growth and progress in order to measure how much you have learned about the ECT process. A simple suggestion would be to use a highlighter or black marker at the end of each chapter to note which sections of the ECT Flowchart you are able to comprehend. In order not to cause undue stress let me emphasizes that oftentimes we do some of the ECT steps automatically or instinctively.

A great way to learn psychology techniques is through storytelling. This book will utilize that approach as it makes learning the process of Emotional Core Therapy even simpler and more enjoyable. For readers who learn through a more interactive style, there will be a list of important concepts at the end of each chapter.

EMOTIONAL CORE THERAPY AND THE SCIENTIFIC METHOD

As you begin the journey to understand the Emotional Core Therapy process please keep in mind the scientific method. The scientific method is a process for creating models of the natural world that can be verified experimentally. The scientific method requires making observations, recording data, and analyzing data in a form that can be duplicated by other scientists. The subject of a scientific experiment has to be observable and reproducible. Observations may be made with the unaided eye or any other apparatus suitable for detecting the desired phenomenon. The apparatus for making a scientific observation has to be comprised of well-known scientific principles. The scientific method requires that theories be testable. If a theory cannot be tested, it cannot be a scientific theory. The scientific method requires and relies on direct evidence. This means evidence that can be directly observed and tested. Scientific experiments are designed to be repeated by other scientists and to demonstrate unequivocally the point they are trying to prove by controlling all the factors that could influence the results.

Source (Scientificpsychic.com/Scientific Method)

Here are the four steps to the scientific method and the Emotional Core Therapy process.

1). Observation made both visually and with scientific equipment

Stress affects both the mind and body. There exists a cause and effect relationship with stress. Oftentimes this stress can be uncomfortable for humans.

2) Formulation of a hypothesis to explain the phenomenon in the form of a causal mechanism/method/approach.

Many psychology methods (REBT, CBT, ACT, DBT, etc.), religious approaches (Buddhism, 12 steps, etc.), and educational programs (Smart Recovery) have attempted to fully and completely explain via a model, how this cause and effect relationship with stress occurs. Up until this point in time, we have not had a model in the world that can successfully depict how this stress occurs each and every time. To their credit, many of these methods partially work and have contributed greatly to humanity. See Wiki.com for information on all the psychology methods and techniques mentioned in this book. With the invention/discovery of Emotional Core Therapy (ECT) we now have a psychology method that accurately can depict this causal relationship between stress and humans through my Eight Step Emotional Core Therapy Flowchart. With ECT, we now have a psychology approach that identifies and treats the root cause of psychological stress. The root cause is the temporary arousal of one of the four true emotions (joy, grief, fear, and relief). ECT also shares and borrows many psychological techniques from the aforementioned approaches.

3) Test the hypothesis.

I have tested the Eight Step Flowchart thousands of times in many venues including my clinical practice as well as training other professionals. The ECT process works accurately to depict the situational stress affecting humans. Anytime someone experiences psychological stress, aspects of each of the eight steps of the Emotional Core Therapy Flowchart will be utilized and affected. Why does this phenomenon happen when one experiences stress? The Emotional Core Therapy process highlights and identifies the key components of the root cause of stress. Anyone can test the model which is utilized extensively in this book.

4) Establish a theory based on repeated verification of the results.

Billions of people suffering relationship stress can be helped by Emotional Core Therapy. Every effort needs to be made to ensure people plagued by stress have access to this model and the accompanying treatment program in this book. Every effort needs to be made to educate the human population on the ECT process as all humans suffer stress from time to time. Because of the inclusiveness of Emotional Core Therapy, many effective psychology techniques that have been demonstrated to release stress can be incorporated into ECT. It takes time and will to learn and apply ECT. There are certain exceptions, of course, and those with long-term physical or psychological damage may not be able to utilize all steps effectively.

One of the most powerful benefits of ECT is its ability to incorporate any psychology or religious method that can successfully release emotions. The following approaches are some of the many techniques that have been shown to successfully release emotions. Gestalt Therapy, role playing, psychodrama, art therapy, music therapy, hypnosis, EMDR, biofeedback, Reiki, pet therapy, journaling, Mindfulness, some aspects of prayer, yoga, verbalization of emotions, etc., as part of the eight step process. View Wiki.com for detailed explanations of these techniques. Humans release stress in many ways and it is important to work from a person's worldview and utilize techniques that may be familiar to them.

The ECT process works just like entering data into a computer. You enter your own situational stress into the Emotional Core Therapy Model to relieve stress and get back to a peaceful centered sense of well-being. Relationship stress generally varies from person to person which is step one of the ECT Model. Generally, each individual experiences the four true feelings differently which is step six of the ECT model. People release their stress in a variety of ways which is step seven of the ECT model. And finally, everyone meditates/relaxes in a variety of ways which is step eight of the process. Because of the many varied ways human beings experience and release stress, this book offers you the reader a user friendly approach to effectively treat the stress in your own life.

ECT Flow Chart

Relationships;
self, other people, places, things

⬇

Needs;
emotional, financial, spiritual, physical

⬇

Five Senses;
seeing, touching, smelling, tasting, hearing

⬇

Four Authentic Feelings;
joy, grief, fear, relief

⬇

Effects;
brain/central nervous system

⬇

Uncomfortable Symptoms;
muscle tightness, fatigue, etc.

⬇

Releasing Process;
learn to discharge toxic feelings

⬇

Balancing Your Equilibrium;
practice various daily meditative techniques

INTRODUCTION

This book is about you. Yes, we're all individuals and we have plenty of differences, but what you'll learn here applies to all of us regardless of age, gender, religious beliefs or anything else that sometimes separates people. That's because every single one of us, at one point or another will struggle with problems. But if you don't know how to properly deal with them, things can quickly go from bad to worse. Emotional Core Therapy (ECT) will show you a better way for handling your problems and having a happier life. As a therapist I've been using it very successfully for many years. What's even cooler is that you can learn how to use it to help yourself, and it fits in perfectly with virtually every religious and spiritual belief that may or may not play an important role in your life.

My approach to therapy is to first make sure that people realize that an anguished mind is every bit as painful (sometimes more so) than a hurting body. You would of course go to the doctor if you had a broken leg or a sore throat, right? But for some reason when it comes to the mind people (teenagers especially) are either embarrassed to admit that they have a problem, or worried that it won't work for them.

It doesn't have to be that way. There is no shame in seeking out help. In fact, it is courageous. Will treatment work? Well, in using Emotional Core Therapy, I've come to understand that there is no one "right way" to do therapy. There are lots of great therapists out there, utilizing a wide variety of highly innovative and successful techniques. If I tried to teach all of them, however, it would be overwhelming for the patient. ECT introduces a group of techniques that are simple to do, and they work over time. More importantly, it empowers people to help themselves. If I could teach you the perfect baseball swing, but you could only do it when I am right there standing next to you, what good would that do for you? By the same token, what good is therapy if it doesn't work when you leave the therapist's office? That is a basic premise that I always keep in mind when teaching people about the power that all of us have within ourselves to release our pain and to feel better. ECT has a primary goal of making sure that you can live a life of freedom and independence.

Interestingly enough, most of the world's major religions and spiritual paths share these same goals. Especially as a young person, finding your way in the world can feel like a real challenge sometimes. ECT brings clarity into your life, helping you to better understand yourself. Again, the parallels to religion and spirituality are self-evident. As you continue to mature, these aspects of your life will keep on growing as well.

By learning to monitor your feelings, you can find out what has "hurt" you in life. The basic premise of ECT is to learn from each time that we have debilitating feelings of fear and loss. Let's look at something so simple as putting on a jacket on a cold and blustery day. To protect yourself from the cold, you have to put on layers of clothes to keep warm. I'm sure we all learned that at a young age. In ECT, we do something very similar with our feelings. Harmful feelings of fear and loss can actually endanger your body in much the same way that a snowy and wintry day would surely beat up on you if you dressed only in a T-shirt and shorts.

The goal of ECT is to reduce toxic pain. By the time you finish reading this book you will be so familiar with the process that you will be able to use it whenever you need, just like slipping on that winter jacket whenever the temperature drops. At the heart of Emotional Core Therapy is learning how to identify and process the four authentic feelings that arise from all relationships. They are joy, grief, fear, and relief.

These things are universal to the entire human family. There is no problem in the world that someone else has not experienced. Emotional Core Therapy offers a practical, realistic and very effective method for dealing with all of them. It all begins with honoring your five senses: hearing, seeing, smelling, tasting and touching. Pay close attention to all five of them. What are they telling you? You will never really know if you impair your senses with toxins such as caffeine, drugs, alcohol, lack of sleep, etc. An individual who honors his or senses will be more aware not only of the outside world, but of their own inner world as well. This is the realm of religious and spiritual thinking. For those of you that value faith, ECT will build up your belief system as it strengthens your confidence in yourself. It works just as effectively for those with a more secular (non-religious) outlook, too.

I like to use metaphors. They've been invaluable in forming my understanding of the world in assisting those who come to me for help. I will use them throughout this book. One of my favorites involves golf. A golfer needs to be honest with himself/herself, and decide if their emotions on the course are helping or hurting them. For example, would an aspiring pro golfer who throws his clubs when he misses a drive, be an improved golfer if he handled his emotions properly? Can the proper understanding of emotions lower your score? How many shots does one throw away because of poorly handled emotions? Mastering the psychology of the mind is essential for any amateur or professional golfer who strives to be his best. The idea is to truly be comfortable with one's self as well as learn to identify feelings that are uncomfortable, but sometimes things get a bit more complex.

Let me explain. Consider a golfer that hits four to five excellent shots in a row. To the naked eye, no problem, he is playing well, so he will want to keep the positive vibrations going. Right? Wrong, that is not what the elite golfers do! If they do, they will elevate their central nervous system, and before you know it they will make an errant shot from too much adrenaline. That is why, to the contrary, elite golfers have a calmness about them. Most have learned to maintain a good, balanced psyche. It is also important to realize that it is possible to have too many feelings of joy and relief.

But learning how to process our true feelings and properly handle our emotions not only goes well beyond golf, it actually applies to virtually all of life. Think about it, even without a major crisis, on a day in, day out basis we all have minor psychic pain of one sort or another. It could be a difficult to live with parent, a boss with a short fuse, a girlfriend or boyfriend who is always "pushing your buttons," etc. Though not debilitating, these daily irritants can build up and steal away your happiness and peace of mind. As you become more aware of your feelings, you will be better able to decide what you can handle and what you cannot. It may need to involve terminating certain relationships. For example, if a class you are taking is so awful that you are living in misery, the only solution might be to drop it and enroll in a new class. But there are also other techniques that can be used for identifying and releasing feelings, as we will see.

Of course, you have to use prudence and common sense too. If at any point you ever feel that you might be a danger to yourself or other people, you may need to either call 911 or check into a hospital Emergency Room. Though common and universal to all people, normally mild ailments such as sadness, anxiety and anger can sometimes be serious enough to require hospitalization. In every situation, err on the side of caution, as it's always better to be safe than sorry.

To help explain the many benefits of Emotional Core Therapy I want for you to imagine a rudderless rowboat rowing down the river. What does it take for a rowboat to traverse down the waterway? Fuel of course. In this case, fuel would consist of a healthy diet. By that we mean not using stimulants such as coffee, caffeinated soda, and excess sugar, all of which affect the central nervous system. All stimulants or depressants affect the four authentic feelings of joy, grief, fear, and relief. Minor uses such as a cup of coffee in the morning or salt on your popcorn, likely would not affect a person's central nervous system in a chronic manner. The best advice I can give here is to speak with your family doctor if you have concerns with your dietary intake. The important factor to remember is that food and drink can have a positive or negative impact on your central nervous system. Although the topic of food intake is beyond the scope of this book, just keep in mind that the relationship exists.

Back to our rudderless rowboat…it's gliding through the water effortlessly and smoothly. Try and visualize the peaceful state of the rowboat as it courses downstream. Soft, tranquil yet very sturdy. Quite a vessel, wouldn't you say? Now imagine if this rudderless rowboat was able to traverse the sea and ocean for months and years in the same manner. What an enjoyable experience. This is ideally, the emotional state of a person who has successfully learned ECT. Even if a person never read a word about ECT, they could have this same feeling. How? By just staying emotionally balanced and healthy their whole lives. Sounds like a fun and enjoyable way of life. So what is so hard about achieving this state? Rather than give you the answer, let's realistically explore what happens to people as they experience life using the rudderless rowboat example.

Now, with our rowboat traveling the waterways, what happens from time to time? Bad weather conditions affect our sturdy little vessel. High winds and rain, along with cold and hot temperatures seriously call into question the reliability of the boat to keep out water. From time to time, a big wave (rainstorm) causes water to leak into the rowboat. Consequently, the rowboat slows down and its power is weakened. If a tornado or hurricane passes in the path of the rowboat, you can be slowed to a near stop. This is in effect, what happens to teenagers when the relationships they are in go sour. Their vitality and vigor for life becomes diminished when negative and toxic emotions adversely affect them. Recall how it feels when you lose a close friend who you bonded with for several years, or any other human tragedy. Well, that devastation that you felt is similar to what has happened to someone aboard this fictionalized boat.

As Emotional Core Therapy explains, it is the entering and leaving of relationships that can cause tension and stress in our lives. Examine the list below of commonly occurring stressful events in life that can cause debilitating feelings of fear and loss.

1. Death of a family member including grandparents/ parents/sibling/etc.
2. Divorce or separation of parents
3. Major health problem such as cancer, diabetes, etc.
4. Being fired or reprimanded at work

5. Problems or disputes with relatives or close friends
6. Pregnancy
7. Being bullied at school
8. Failing grades at school
9. Catching your boyfriend or girlfriend cheating
10. Parents having to relocate for their job
11. Spilt or breakup with boyfriend/girlfriend
12. Changing your high school or college plans
13. Major weather disaster such as hurricane or tornado
14. Loss of important leisure or sports activity due to injury
15. Being harassed at school
16. Loss of home due to parents' economic hardship
17. Long standing disagreements with parent or other family member
18. Getting in trouble with the law
19. Change in health of close friend or family member
20. Close friends move out of state/out of town

Any one of the above stressful events would cause any human being to suffer. The real difference is that emotionally healthy people, including those practicing ECT, appropriately process their feelings. If this includes embracing your religious or spiritual beliefs strongly, you might even consider ECT as a gift from God. Just remember, like any good gift, it is only going to be helpful if you consistently use it!

The most common state of a person that successfully has learned ECT is one of tranquillity and a balanced equilibrium. Meditation helps a great deal in this regard. It is one of the highest forms of self-care or self-love, and is critical to healthy development. As a culture, we need to do more to support the individual's need to take care of oneself/love oneself. This is especially important for teens, because many times they have not been taught how to bring themselves to a reflective / meditative state. The good news is, there are literally hundreds of ways to meditate – and the benefits are amazing!

When one is very comfortable with this loving/meditative lifestyle they can truly defend themselves from society's pressures which are bombarding them day in and day out. How can this be achieved? Over time, your body can become readily able to identify foreign feelings such as joy, grief, fear, and relief. As a therapist I often tell my clients to embrace toxic feelings of fear and grief! Why? They (debilitating feelings) are telling you that something is wrong. While these feelings affect all of us, the fact of the matter is, joy, grief, fear, or relief does not dominate an emotionally healthy person. These four authentic feelings are just temporary states that affect the person from time to time. Let's face it, a perfectly smooth running rowboat does not exist. It is not realistic. What is realistic is that one can expect some minor water coming in from time to time. In rare instances, a rushing torrent of flooding water threatens to sink the rowboat – a perfect analogy for when we need to seek out professional help. Every community has some really awesome therapists, social workers, doctors, etc. who have dedicated their lives to helping people just like you. If you need them, don't ever hesitate to seek them out. After all, that is what they are there for.

An emotionally healthy person practicing ECT is committed to a life of having peace and comfort in their day. Their mind is allowed to daydream and reflect. Reflection is key as it is a relaxed way the mind can roam and wander from thought to thought in an effortless manner. The bottom line is, there is just no substitute for taking time for yourself daily. It is a way of respecting yourself to allow yourself, the time to be rested and peaceful. Here is a list of 40 popular ways to relax:

1. Exercise before school, get the blood flowing
2. Practice yoga, Pilates, or chi gong
3. Reduce the amount of caffeine you drink (especially soda!)
4. Go for a run around the block when you have some free time at home
5. Practice deep breathing throughout the day
6. Get your daily chores out of the way now instead of worrying about them
7. Cut out the excess sugar in your diet (it causes stress)
8. Throw out stuff around your house / bedroom you really don't need or use
9. Do some gardening in the yard
10. Get some fresh air by taking a brisk nature walk
11. Go for a quick swim at the local pool
12. Do some deep muscle stretches

13. Practice sewing or needlework

14. Go somewhere where sunlight warms your face

15. Call some old friends and spend some time hanging out and catching up on things

16. Tidy your room and make your bed so it's clean when you go to sleep

17. Head down to the beach and walk in shallow water

18. Escape by reading a relaxing book

19. Take some allotted time to do nothing at all

20. Go to bed early

21. Drink some lemon tea or green tea

22. Take a day off from your after-school job (with the boss' permission of course!)

23. Go and see a comedy show

24. Get a neck or a foot massage

25. Go for a walk around the markets or somewhere with lots of natural produce

26. Ride a bike in nature

27. Go red light tanning

28. Get off the computer and relax your eyes

29. Listen to some classic rock

30. Play a sport such as pickup basketball or bowling with friends just for fun

31. Watch a movie or TV show

32. Say a reflective prayer over and over in a relaxed chant

33. Sing to yourself in a humming or relaxed manner

34. Journal, draw or paint your random thoughts

35. Watch your thoughts without engaging them

36. Go fishing or boating

37. Spend some time with your dog or other animal

38. Pick up a hobby you have neglected

39. Let your imagination wander with some vacation you'd love to take in the future

40. Go out to a favorite restaurant for dinner

OK, at this point, you may be saying, thanks for that great list, but really, why would someone possibly write another self-help book? After all, ECT sounds interesting, but there are many excellent psychology books out there that do a great job at highlighting specific psychology techniques. So why add yet another book?

First and foremost, people are still suffering emotional trauma day in and day out. Look at America's prison system. We have several million people incarcerated in our jails and prisons, with millions of others on probation or parole. On top of that, we have thousands of people in psychiatric hospitals. Moreover, we have millions of people who are in so much pain that they are either under a doctor's care, or are self-medicating through illegal drugs or alcohol to numb the pain. It's a gigantic national problem.

Much of this pain can be avoided with proper care of one's emotional health. That is why I think it is so important for people to learn the techniques of Emotional Core Therapy, especially at a young age, which is the primary purpose of this book. It is a way to take care of yourself in a preventive manner. Think about all of the other self-care techniques that you employ every day. Taking a shower and brushing your teeth for example. Both of these daily habits help keep disease away. ECT is also a daily habit, that when used correctly can help maintain one's health. Even better, it is so simple that normal everyday people can practice the technique. No special training required!

Is ECT the only route to mental health? Not at all. As we said, there are lots of other partially effective therapies and plenty of good self-help books out there. There is also the strong guidance of parents, mentors and religious leaders in your community to help you. But ECT does tackle, head on, the fact that relationships, toxic or harmful, are a part of life for everyone. They are unavoidable. The only thing you can really do is to educate yourself on what is a healthy relationship. A healthy relationship can only begin if one is emotionally healthy. A healthy or stable person, as seen through the lens of ECT is a person who has full awareness of the four authentic feelings, joy, grief, fear, and relief. Furthermore, a healthy person knows how to live a relaxed and meditative lifestyle.

A healthy relationship is built on mutual respect. The communication style is one of openness and honesty. Lying and stealing are not part of a healthy relationship. Being able to trust and share one's authentic feelings is paramount to a healthy relationship. One can only do this if the relationship allows for a caring atmosphere to exist where all feelings are welcomed and understood. This means that one has to be able to share feelings of fear and loss as well as joy and relief.

One of the most important benefits of Emotional Core Therapy is that you begin to examine why particular relationships cause you debilitating feelings. This enables you to learn from your relationships and make better "relationship choices" next time. You begin to empower yourself by identifying and participating in healthy relationships, which in turn leads to more hope for the future.

This book about Emotional Core Therapy is meant as a teaching tool. That is why we use the approach of storytelling – it is a great way to teach as you can learn through others' experience in a joyful, non-threatening manner.

The alternative, simply ignoring our emotional needs or seeking relief in unhealthy ways, can prove disastrous. Oftentimes people begin to learn inappropriate self-soothing techniques and bad habits in their teens. My hope is that by writing in a short, storytelling, easy to read style, you will avoid these and start to learn to process your feelings in a safe and healthy manner.

Is ECT guaranteed to solve our problems, and how long does it take? First of all, nobody can guarantee anything in this life. All we can say regarding ECT is that it has proven to be a very effective and successful approach. But time and will (motivation) are needed for this approach to fully work. Why? Mature relationships – friends, school, boyfriend / girlfriend, etc. – frequently require the needs of others to be met. Even our own needs often have to be met in relationships. Whether it's emotional, financial, spiritual, or physical, humans are often required or asked to meet the needs of others in relationships. A key point of ECT is the concept of working to meet the needs of one's self or others in relationships.

As we begin to discuss the benefits of ECT we need to point out that some people may have to work longer and harder to reap these benefits. There are individuals who have impairments with one or more of their five senses (seeing, touching, smelling, tasting, and hearing). These impairments can cause their feelings of joy, grief, fear, and relief to be adversely affected. For example, a visually impaired person may not receive the same response watching a movie at the theatre as a non-visually impaired person. Also, there are individuals who have suffered severe early childhood trauma that is permanent in nature. For example, a child suffering from fetal alcohol syndrome may have some sensory problems that affect the ability to sense and feel. It is not that some of the benefits of Emotional Core Therapy will not be utilized, but the desired outcome of learning ECT may be harder than usual.

What other situations would arise that would cause ECT to not be successful? This book outlines situations and exceptions to where ECT may not have success. Like all treatment approaches people have to be comfortable with the process. Having the book told in a "simple storytelling fashion" is a means that has been successful with other psychological techniques, and I hope and trust that you will find it very helpful here as well.

So if you're ready to finally love yourself to the core, to love yourself enough to care for yourself emotionally in ways that will improve your life forever, keep reading. You're in for a spiritual journey that will forever transform the quality of your being.

All identifiable information about actual clients has been changed to protect patient confidentiality. Moreover, all the cases mentioned in this book can be assumed to be fictional. Mr. Moylan treats all of his clients, religious and secular, with the same empathy and compassion. His ECT model strives to work from each client's particular worldview. Some cases are hypothetical and are used as a teaching tool.

ECT Flow Chart

Relationships;
self, other people, places, things

Needs;
emotional, financial, spiritual, physical

Five Senses;
seeing, touching, smelling, tasting, hearing

Four Authentic Feelings;
joy, grief, fear, relief

Effects;
brain/central nervous system

Uncomfortable Symptoms;
muscle tightness, fatigue, etc.

Releasing Process;
learn to discharge toxic feelings

Balancing Your Equilibrium;
practice various daily meditative techniques

CHAPTER ONE
How ECT Works

One of the most incredible things about being human is how many emotions we have. Emotions, also called "feelings," have an effect on everything you do every single day. Imagine if you had better control over your emotions – if you understood them and knew how to deal with them more effectively. Think that would improve things in your life? Of course it would, which is why looking at the "big picture" is such a good place to start. First of all, how many names for emotions are there? It's hard to pin an exact number to it, but there are hundreds of them at the very least. Here is just a partial list of some of the many ways that we express ourselves:

1. Loving
2. Wonderful
3. Joyous
4. Happy
5. Peaceful

6. Satisfied
7. Ecstatic
8. Content
9. Serene
10. Pleased
11. Elated
12. Excited
13. Overjoyed
14. Glad
15. Festive
16. Thrilled
17. Enthusiastic
18. Eager
19. Cheerful
20. Optimistic
21. Anxious
22. Fearful
23. Tormented
24. Nervous
25. Pessimistic
26. Depressed
27. Helpless
28. Disappointed
29. Upset
30. Bitter
31. Frustrated
32. Inflamed
33. Incensed

34. Tense

35. Irritated

36. Skeptical

37. Unsure

38. Rejected

39. Offended

40. Heartbroken

I'm sure you could add a lot more of your own, but you get the point. People are feeling emotions all the time and they can spell the difference between the best day you've ever had and the absolute worst. Not to mention everything in between. It sounds complicated, but with Emotional Core Therapy these hundreds of different feelings can all be broken down, or categorized into one of *four authentic feelings*. These are **joy, grief, fear, and relief.** Remember these! They are the key. Once you've learned how to identify them, so many things that once left you scratching your head will now seem crystal clear.

It's also important to understand the role that stress plays in your life. Teenagers live with a huge amount of stress on a daily basis. Take a minute to think about all of the many things in your everyday life that cause you stress. Sometimes just thinking about all of that stress is stressful! Unfortunately, there is no magic formula for completely eliminating stress from your life. That's impossible. Each new day brings with it the possibility of stressful situations. Consider, for example, all of the stress that is involved in

competitive sports (whether as a spectator or a partici-
pant). Athletics involve experiencing all four of the "four
authentic feelings." Again, these are joy, grief, fear and
relief. Watch or play just about any sport and it won't take
long before you recognize one or (more likely) all four of
these feelings popping up. As a therapist, my main focus
in counseling athletes and all of my other clients is to have
them understand these four authentic feelings.

In simple terms all four true or authentic feelings evolve
from entering and leaving relationships. OK, what the heck
does that mean? Don't get confused by the word "relationships." Used in the context of ECT, it doesn't necessarily have
anything to do with "romantic" relationships (which is probably what you assumed). Think of it instead more in terms of
entering or leaving different situations, as you will see from
some of the examples below.

Let's take a look at the following diagram.

Flow Chart of Four Primary Feelings

Joy   Grief

Something
You
Like,
Pleasurable
Activity

Fear/Anxiety   Relief

Something
You
Dislike,
Unpleasurable
Activity

As you can see from this diagram, when you go towards something you like there is "Joy". What is Joy? In simple terms, it is a pleasurable state of arousal. If you ask someone, "what makes you joyful?" they will probably describe a relationship they are happy about entering into. An example would be seeing your favorite sports team win a close game. Another example would be hugging a loved one or someone you admire. Do you now see what I mean by "entering into a relationship"?

On the other hand, when you leave a relationship that you enjoyed, the result is grief. For example, leaving your warm, cozy house on a rainy day. Or it might be saying good-bye to your dog when you go off to school in the morning.

This diagram also shows what happens when you enter a relationship that you dislike. A relationship that you dislike will provoke feelings of fear. Imagine climbing inside a cage with a hungry lion. Entering into that relationship would no doubt make you experience fear! The same goes for jumping into the ocean if you don't know how to swim.

But what happens when you leave a situation that you dislike? There is relief. You escape out of the cage and slam the door on that hungry lion that wanted you for a snack. Or you finally reach the shore – and kiss the dry ground – after almost drowning in the ocean. These are great examples of relief!

This flowchart of four authentic feelings is critical to understanding Emotional Core Therapy. Feel free to go ahead and test it for yourself. All you have to do is substitute several of your own relationship experiences for those that we have listed here. Try a bunch for each authentic feeling and you will see exactly how these feelings are influencing throughout the day.

As the ECT Flowchart below highlights, it is relationships that spark the four authentic feelings in us. Specifically, relationships with our selves or others usually involve needs being met. For the sake of simplicity, I organize needs into four categories. Emotional, financial, spiritual, and physical. The benefit of ECT is that it helps you to easily identify your feelings, which gives you incredible control over your own life, as you learn how to release these feelings in an appropriate way. It helps get you into a calm, meditative frame of mind that is free from stress.

ECT Flow Chart

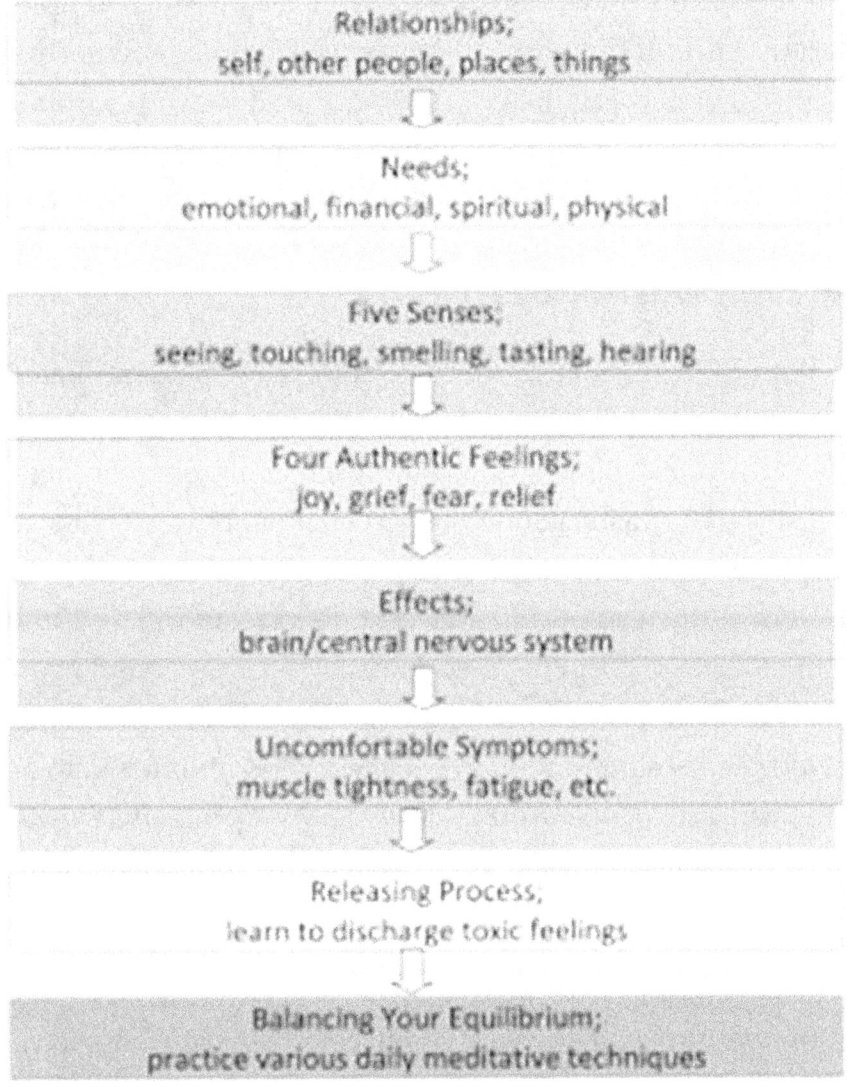

Relationships;
self, other people, places, things

⬇

Needs;
emotional, financial, spiritual, physical

⬇

Five Senses;
seeing, touching, smelling, tasting, hearing

⬇

Four Authentic Feelings;
joy, grief, fear, relief

⬇

Effects;
brain/central nervous system

⬇

Uncomfortable Symptoms;
muscle tightness, fatigue, etc.

⬇

Releasing Process;
learn to discharge toxic feelings

⬇

Balancing Your Equilibrium;
practice various daily meditative techniques

After studying the ECT flowchart several times, I want you to envision a particularly traumatic event in your life. Did your experience resemble the sequence highlighted in the eight step ECT flowchart? If so, in what way? If not, do not worry. We have the entire book to help you learn the ECT process.

You might be surprised to discover how easily and appropriately ECT fits in with all kinds of religious and spiritual beliefs. Developing a calm, peaceful relationship with God goes hand in hand with learning the techniques of ECT. You certainly don't have to be religious to learn any of this, but if you are it will in all likelihood become a part of your spiritual life and make it even stronger.

With ECT, you can continue to fully participate in whatever religious practices you and your family already adhere to and observe. Indeed, the countless support mechanisms of religious and spiritual organizations have been helping teenagers and young adults for centuries in many different areas of life. When you look at the careers of successful people you will find that a large number of them received spiritual guidance in their youth and / or were active in religious groups. Your local church, synagogue, mosque, etc. is an excellent place to meet kind and compassionate people who understand your problems and concerns and would be glad to offer you their wisdom and guidance. When you think about it, what a shame it would be to let such awesome resources go to waste.

By the same token ECT requires no specialized ceremonies, formulaic prayers or profession of faith. Instead, the focus is on "quieting" your mind so that you are calm, peaceful and open to fully embrace the spirituality that you were brought up with that is part of your life and who you are.

The basics of ECT are simple to understand and to apply. When you enter a relationship that you like there is joy (remember, this is not limited to relationships with other people, as it could be many things; think of eating your favorite ice cream). When you leave something that you like there is grief (saying good-bye to someone you love – or finishing off the ice cream). When you go towards something you dislike there is fear. Imagine walking near a snake pit. When you leave a fearful event, there is relief (running away from that snake pit as fast as you can should do the trick).

Have you ever played sports? Well, then you know, the tougher your opponent, the tougher the test is for you emotionally. Grief (otherwise known as loss) and fear (otherwise known as anxiety) are the two most debilitating feelings that all athletes face when they play. In some cases, every game that you play is filled with these unwanted feelings. For example, if you're a football player you maybe start feeling anxiety every Friday afternoon during the fall, simply because you know that you will be playing in a game later that night. The point is, whatever your sport, at every level you need to get a handle on your emotions before game time rolls around – or face the consequences.

Hopefully, this is all starting to make sense to you. Yet, you very well might be asking, "Well, that's great for sports… but what about everything else in life?" My answer: there is no area of life where ECT will not be able to help you. We all need to find healthy ways to process our emotions every single day, wherever we are and whatever we are doing. It doesn't matter how old you are, your financial circumstances, your love life or anything else. Your emotions are always there. They are an essential part of who you are. It makes no sense to try to bury them or to ignore them. Even if you could, you wouldn't want to, when you think about how lame and boring it would be to live in a world without feelings. Some people try, through drugs, alcohol and countless other means – but they inevitably end up harming themselves and lots of other people in the process. That's because they never learned a healthier way to cope with "toxic" feelings. Think of ECT as a lifestyle choice that will improve your mental health.

Like any lifestyle change, what you learn through ECT will not take root overnight, but over the course of weeks, months or years. It has to become a part of your everyday life, and in the process it will help your life to be more centered. How? By starting with the reality that grief and fear are an inevitable for all of us. You already know that's true, so why not equip yourself for something so common in life? Learning ECT is easier than it looks.

The real work of this book is to understand six major concepts (understanding relationships, understanding various needs being met, authentic feelings, mind and body distress, releasing feelings, and dutiful meditation). Two other concepts (the role of our five senses, and the central nervous system being affected) occur quite quickly and without much thinking, but we will still examine them more closely in the final chapter.

Part of the overall ECT process we do instinctively anyway! For example, we enter and leave relationships all day long. So this is really not all that difficult for us to understand and follow. If you allow yourself the time to learn ECT, and are willing to commit the process to memory, you will very soon begin to see the results. Emotional Core Therapy is learning a process that will increase your enthusiasm and appreciation for life.

In order for ECT to be of real value, you need to be able to commit it to your long-term memory, which only happens through repetitious work.

How Memory Works

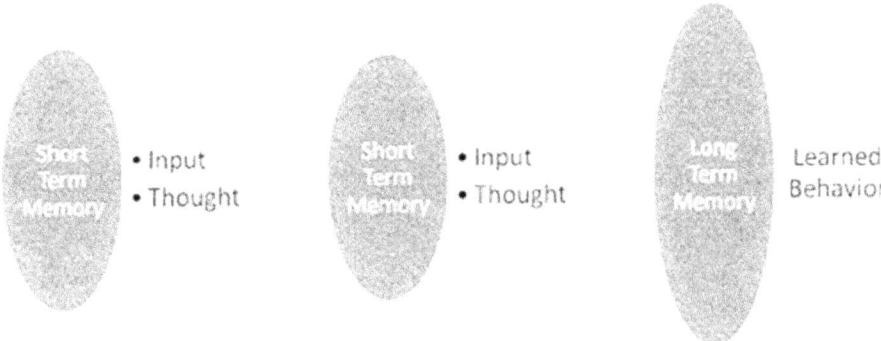

| Short Term Memory | • Input • Thought | Short Term Memory | • Input • Thought | Long Term Memory | Learned Behavior |

The goal is to never forget the process of how emotions work. We spend a year in high school learning Algebra, which many of us forget a few years later. That's OK if we go on to careers that never require Algebra. But we will always have emotions! So why not learn a process of emotional healing that will serve us our entire lives no matter where we live or what we do?

All of us humans know our dates of birth, our race, ethnicity, religion, etc. Why? We know these facts about ourselves because we learned them over and over again when were young. It takes time and energy to learn these important pieces of information about our life. In other words, practice, practice, practice. This information is useful and necessary as it serves to ground and center us as human beings.

Another way to understand how memory works is to think about Driver's Ed. Maybe you just got your driver's license, or will be doing so soon. How do you go about achieving this very important goal? When learning how to drive a car, you need to master certain things, and memory and repetition play a big role. Once you finally get that license, driving your own car opens up the world for you and you no longer feel restricted like you once did. The same goes for ECT.

Emotional Core Therapy is also an approach that will allow you to be centered in life. As ECT explains, grief and fear are an inevitable part of life. In any given year it is likely that one in five people will experience something that is emotionally devastating to them. Why not equip yourself for something so common in life? You will find an ECT Flowchart at the beginning of the book and at the end of each chapter as a reference point. This allows you to gauge how much you have learned about ECT after reading a chapter. A checkpoint of key ECT issues lets you focus on key concepts at a leisurely pace.

Let's now examine how the four authentic feelings are processed. It is our senses – seeing, touching, smelling, tasting, and hearing – that process of all of our feelings. As a therapist, over the years I have found that focusing on the release of authentic feelings has been helpful for clients' growth and development. Imagine that you are caught outside in a violent thunderstorm. If you are like most people you would get overwhelmed by emotions and lunge for the nearest umbrella. ECT, when practiced effectively, can downgrade a severe thunderstorm to just some minor drizzle. Emotional Core Therapy is effective because it filters out ambiguous words and negative thoughts by emphasizing and understanding the four true and authentic feelings.

It all begins with learning to continually monitor the four feelings. This approach offers hope even for those who have suffered the worst possible cases of trauma and abuse. Traumatic and stressful events, as most everybody unfortunately knows, come in a wide variety of shapes and sizes. The good news is that ECT is a helpful treatment option because it empowers you to assess your problems in a simple, yet effective manner.

The goal of Emotional Core Therapy is to get clients to be as peaceful and emotionally centered as a healthy two-year old. The definition of having a peaceful, relaxing, and meditative state is to feel non-threatened, or effected, by the four authentic feelings. Envision an infant in a crib, smiling and relaxed. Just as an infant can sit in a crib in a blissful state, a teen or an adult can also achieve a calm and relaxed state of being. As you read this book you will learn techniques to achieve meditation throughout the day. Meditation, a calm state of being, is essential for the successful use of Emotional Core Therapy, and makes it much easier to identify the four authentic feelings. It is crucial for people to learn at a young age how to love themselves. Only when you truly love yourself can you begin to control your destiny as a human being. ECT teaches us how to love ourselves by properly identifying what it means to be an "Emotional" human being.

One technique that many of my clients have found helpful is the concept of mindfulness. This is a method of keeping oneself in the present moment rather than letting fear and depressing thoughts pre-occupy your thinking. Mindfulness makes an excellent fit with the approach and goals of ECT. As a matter of fact, the more a person learns about ECT, the more he or she will come to understand that such meditation can bring a sense of stillness and quietude to the mind that helps enormously in one's daily life.

Mindfulness is a highly effective technique to calm the central nervous system down. It not only involves the mind, but the body as well. While sitting in a comfortable chair, you concentrate only on your breathing, in and out slowly through your nostrils, feeling the gentle rise and fall of your abdomen. If your thoughts begin to wander, all you need to do is to return them to the simple act of breathing.

Even better, a similar but small variation of mindfulness can be custom-tailored for each individual. With every ECT client, regardless of age, we try to find what has worked in the past and what each client is comfortable in doing as a meditation exercise. This can involve prayer, meditation or a number of other methods. It's important to remember that a meditative lifestyle and state of being, is the eighth step of the ECT Flowchart. We may not always be able to achieve this goal on a day to day basis, but the more we make an effort to stay calm and relaxed and make mental health a priority in life, the better chance we have of identifying stress.

To illustrate why this is so important, consider for a moment a high school senior named Charlie who is getting ready to take his ACT test. He is taking his ACT prep class along with Advanced Placement Chemistry and Honors English. Charlie is overwhelmed (ECT defines this as too much fear or excessive fear). He is also exhausted and has had trouble sleeping. It's clear that he needs to regain himself – but how? We view any type of relaxation or meditative state that allows you to reflect and daydream as a way to self-care or love oneself.

In Charlie's case, he was able to daydream by shooting baskets in his driveway. Whenever he had his basketball in his hands it served as a way for Charlie to rejuvenate his body and release the stress that comes with schoolwork. Of course, shooting baskets or hoops will not work for everyone. Another boy may like drawing or sketching, while a different kid may like hanging out by the pool. The key point to remember is to keep this reflective state throughout the day so that you can identify and release the four authentic feelings of joy, grief, fear and relief.

Many people suffering from grief or fear (which, as we said, is also known as anxiety) come to my office in a sad state of affairs with little hope of feeling better. Emotional Core Therapy teaches techniques to help yourself learn how to process emotions properly, and in ways that are healthy rather than destructive. Remember that *the four authentic feelings ultimately all stem from either entering or leaving relationships.* Take, for example, a boy and a girl who are having a strained relationship. The real problem is that they both have to grow and learn about each other. With ECT, we pay attention to how each feels in the relationship. The girlfriend (Ashley) in this scenario tells the therapist, "I get scared when Brandon comes over to do homework and hang out with me some afternoons. I know that he works hard at school during the day. He's taking the SAT soon and I know it's been making him tense. Still, I cringe when he comes over because he's so stressed out that any little thing that I might say wrong can set him off and start a big argument."

With ECT, we focus on the meaning of her feelings. In this case, both words she uses, "scared" and "cringe" are different vocabulary names for the authentic feeling, "Fear".

What Ashley is saying is that this relationship she has entered into brings fear into her life from time to time. She is not saying that they have a terrible relationship. She just wants to work towards a better resolution in this particular situation.

It is very hard to live life with unwanted and toxic feelings. Moreover, holding back (or holding in) your feelings can be very harmful in the long term. ECT utilizes a wide variety of commonly known techniques to release feelings. One of the most popular is to "verbalize" one's feelings. By talking out your fears with a compassionate therapist, toxic feelings such as fear (otherwise known as anxiety) are released. This is called catharsis. That's a big word, but basically it simply means a cleansing of the soul. With ECT, we are vigilant about cleansing our soul. Just like you learned to brush your teeth and wash your hands as a daily habit when you were a little kid, your soul also needs this type of positive treatment.

There are other ways that Ashley can learn to cleanse her soul. She can journal, listen to music, exercise, meditate, etc. Throughout the book you will find examples of releasing techniques. If for example Ashley had come in with lots of complaints of fear/anxiety because she is afraid to confront her boyfriend for not listening to her, I may focus on her learning to be more assertive with her needs. In this example, the first step is identifying the fear.

This is similar to a young man on the high school basketball team who says that he has a panic attack every time he has to go to the line for a free throw. He has excess fear, which adversely affects his concentration. This leads to his shot being messed up of course, because he needs to be free of tension and smooth to be effective. When an athlete in any sport lets his feelings have a negative effect on his performance it is called "choking". In other words, his nerves get in his way. The smart solution is to let a coach and perhaps a therapist help him through his emotional problem. Both of them will be supportive, caring, and allow an environment for the student athlete to take risks, and to make changes if necessary. Do you see how this is similar to a girl suffering fear from her boyfriend? That's precisely why, when I use Emotional Core Therapy I encourage clients to take risks and make changes if they are suffering debilitating feelings of fear and loss.

Another example might involve a teenage girl who has to take care of her two young brothers after school every day. She tells her therapist, "I just feel so overwhelmed by them, and I hate that I sometimes yell or get angry at them." Clearly, she chose her words carefully. She used the word "overwhelmed" because the reality is that she has too much fear! She's fearful (worried, concerned...feel free to add your own) that she will "fail" to fully or adequately complete all of the many tasks and responsibilities expected of her by her parents. The solution, then, is that she needs to be organized and structured in such a way so that she can feel a sense of accomplishment for the important contribution that she is making for her busy family (both parents work outside the home all day).

The teen girl's name is Marsha and she had been raised with solid traditional Christian values. Her parents and her faith had instilled in her a feeling of obligation when it came to helping out with the family. Marsha would constantly ask herself the question, "What would Jesus do?" and the answer was always that He would help out with the youngsters without complaining. But Marsha did complain. Not aloud, but inside of her own mind. And the pressure that Marsha put on herself because of it led to debilitating feelings of guilt.

We all get overwhelmed from time to time. The dictionary definition of "overwhelming" is overpowering in effect or strength. Let's consider what is really happening to this young lady in terms of the four authentic feelings. Without a doubt, she is moving towards someone or something she does not like. Let me be clear, I am not saying that she does not like her young brothers. In fact, part of her fear is that, because she loves them so much, she's desperately afraid of failing both them and her parents. She fears that she might not be up to the task, however, because it includes so many things that worry her. For example, she may love to ride bicycles with her brothers. But then the two boys invite their two friends, meaning that their older sister is now responsible for four kids. What then happens if they ride their bicycles near a busy street? The situation, she fears, could very easily spin out of control. What was once manageable and enjoyable, is now overwhelming.

Emotional Core Therapy will help Marsha by isolating the problem, assessing the cause, and providing appropriate relief. We see that additional fear creeps into her thinking about this new activity when more children are involved, and in a more dangerous situation. When you have too much fear, it's important to reduce it somehow, if possible. A beneficial approach may be to highlight the new tasks and responsibilities involved in the four children scenario. By focusing on how this girl feels (muscle tension, lack of sleep, headaches, etc.) we can get her to modify her activities with her children. In the future, once she learns the technique, she can utilize ECT in other fearful, stress-inducing situations. Examples might be when she feels too much fear at school, or in other relationships. The point is, once you learn the techniques for processing your four authentic feelings, you will be amazed at how much this knowledge makes fundamental differences (for the better) in your everyday life and in the "big issues" (family, health, relationships, finances, etc.). When I speak of "big issues" I mean "life events". Emotional Core Therapy has the ability, when used correctly, to completely change your outlook on life for the better.

Moreover, since Marsha has a strong Christian faith, to overcome her fears she was able to incorporate prayer right along with ECT. By visualizing a calm, peaceful image of Jesus smiling upon her, her central nervous system began to calm down. At various times of the day, she would recite lengthy prayers like the "Our Father". Though beautiful and heart-felt, such prayers could also have the effect of focusing Marsha's mind on relationships in her life. When focusing on relationships, she would find herself getting a bit stressed.

So, for the purpose of calming her mind, she focused on less thinking, and instead, she simply concentrated her thoughts of peaceful imagery of Jesus.

A picture of Jesus smiling benevolently and wearing flowing white garments that she had received as a gift for her First Communion was particularly soothing when it came to slowing her mind and body down and relaxing. Marsha didn't even need to be looking directly at the picture. The vivid thought imagery that she carried within her mind's eye was more than enough to flood her soul with the peace that she so desired.

With this powerful combination, rather than feeling the pressures of not "letting down" God and her family, Marsha will instead learn how to enter into a relaxed and meditative state, replacing all of that tension with the love of God that she will now be in a much better position to experience and enjoy.

Remember earlier in this chapter we used the analogy of a thunderstorm versus drizzle to show how you can feel less overwhelmed when using ECT? The beauty of this is that we can use it with just about any of life's problematic events. With Emotional Core Therapy we funnel all of these life events into two categories: entering and leaving relationships. Emotional stress is caused by moving towards or away from a relationship you have with a person, place, or thing.

This represents a crucial step in ECT, because you can categorize all of your life events into two categories instead of two hundred, or two thousand. You begin to gain control over the stress. You empower yourself by recognizing that the event is separate from you. You gain confidence that this event is something you chose in your life, and (if you want to) you can leave it, by properly processing your feelings.

As you read the various scenarios of people who have successfully used ECT in their lives, keep referring back to the ECT Flowchart and see if you can identify the steps that are being illustrated in the example. Each story involves people using different steps of the process, and as you become more familiar with ECT, watch how much easier it will be for you to pinpoint exactly which step each character in this book is using.

Let's look at a particularly stressful event in this manner. A young man named Joseph has just accepted a part time job offer at a local store. Once he starts his new position, however, he discovers that his boss is a lunatic. He knows that he cannot work there for very long without undue psychological stress. Even though religious faith has never been a major component of this teen's life, by utilizing Emotional Core Therapy, he does indeed gain new insight into his own life; he recognizes that he has entered into a new relationship with someone. In this case, a new boss. Although Joseph has a great deal of fear related to his current life predicament, he nevertheless feels confident deep down. Why? The boy comes to realize that he is not the problem. Yes, he will have to grieve the loss of quitting and getting a new job. Yet, he knows deep down that these feelings will pass. He recognizes that he can process these feelings appropriately through the various techniques that he has learned in his counseling. Utilizing ECT can allow for this very difficult life event to be manageable for this young man. Even though spirituality may not be high on Joseph's list of priorities right now, God still loves him every bit as much as He does all of His children. He loves and helps His children regardless of their background or religious upbringing. It is the human soul that makes all the difference, as each one of us is a unique individual with thoughts and feelings that deserve to be honored and respected. ECT helped Joseph to understand that as a human being he has a right to be treated fairly, and now he has the tools to find peace in his life even under the worst of circumstances.

Throughout his young life Joseph has come into contact with and made some great friendships with kids of several different religious backgrounds including Muslims, Christians, Hindus and others. But his family has always been secular and rather agnostic when it comes to religion. This works fine for Joseph, and he too goes about life from a secular viewpoint, while remaining perfectly comfortable amongst those with a different perspective.

We are now ready to begin to explore the most commonly occurring emotional stresses in the life of teenagers just like you. In the upcoming chapters we will examine various scenarios which are common to teenagers. We will show how

ECT can be effective in helping teens gain peace and confidence in their lives.

As you read the various scenarios unfolding before your eyes, you can finally begin to learn the benefits of Emotional Core Therapy. In my work as a therapist, the most common psychological issues I see are depression, anxiety/fear issues. Most of these stresses to our equilibrium occur when we are with family, friends, at work, school, or in a relationship with someone of the opposite sex. As you become more and more acclimated to the ECT process, you will begin the healthy journey back home to yourself. Think of the movie, "The Wizard of Oz." The main character, Dorothy, relates to the "Good Witch of the North" at the end of the film, repeating over and over, "There is no place like home." This reassuring chant allows her to leave the fantasy world of Oz and return home to Kansas. This is the mantra that you need to learn to fully comprehend Emotional Core Therapy. Every person is lovable. Every person deserves peace. Every person can overcome their troubled emotional state.

In this book you will also learn how ECT helps young people with religious beliefs to practice their faith even more powerfully. ECT keeps you emotionally well-balanced, which is so important for a rich and vibrant spiritual life. Regardless of your religious background (if any) you will learn how ECT helps with just about any problem life may throw at you, lifting up your spirits as you learn the truth about your emotions as a human being, and how to process them in ways that are healthy and will help you to grow.

Keep in mind that Emotional Core Therapy works if you allow the process to work. If you are willing to make a genuine effort to grow and develop as a human being, what you read in the following pages will be transformational in your life. Over time, ECT will empower you by giving you the confidence that you can overcome any of the major traumatic events in life. There is simply no cure for the emotional trauma that life throws at us from time to time. It is how we respond to these hurtful events that defines us as human beings. ECT will teach you how to strengthen your mind and lift up your spirit.

List Five Alternative Words Used To Describe The Feeling Of "Joy"

A) GLAD

B) HAPPY

1.

2.

3.

4.

5.

Notes:

List Five Alternative Words To Describe The Feeling Of "Grief"

A) DEPRESSED

B) SAD

1.

2.

3.

4.

5.

Notes:

List Five Alternative Words To Describe The Feeling Of "Fear"

A) ANXIETY

B) DREAD

1.

2.

3.

4.

5.

Notes:

List Five Alternative Words Used To Describe The Feeling "Relief"

A) RELAXED

B) REPRIEVE

1.

2.

3.

4.

5.

Notes:

List Five Stressful Relationships (People, Places, Or Things) In Your Life

A) ATTENDING A NEW SCHOOL

B) FRIEND GETTING SICK OR ILL

1.

2.

3.

4.

5.

Notes:

List Five Ways You Can Relax In A Meditative State

A) SWIMMING

B) LISTENING TO MUSIC

1.

2.

3.

4.

5.

Notes:

ECT Flow Chart

Relationships;
self, other people, places, things

⇩

Needs;
emotional, financial, spiritual, physical

⇩

Five Senses;
seeing, touching, smelling, tasting, hearing

⇩

Four Authentic Feelings;
joy, grief, fear, relief

⇩

Effects;
brain/central nervous system

⇩

Uncomfortable Symptoms;
muscle tightness, fatigue, etc.

⇩

Releasing Process;
learn to discharge toxic feelings

⇩

Balancing Your Equilibrium;
practice various daily meditative techniques

CHAPTER TWO
Using ECT to Treat Depression

It's a fact, at some time or another, all of us feel depressed. It's just a part of life. Having a strong religious faith does not inoculate you from this problem. Yes, it may help with your ability to cope with feelings of depression but it will not eliminate it. There are all kinds of reasons why people become depressed, and not all depression is created equal. Sometimes we're just feeling a little bit down, other times the depression can be severe. But the good news is, Emotional Core Therapy offers realistic, creative solutions for almost every form of depression.

Consider what might be a "worst case" kind of depression scenario. We all remember the catastrophic tsunami in Japan, and all of the misery that it brought to so many people. Imagine being a teenager in a hard hit area of Japan. When the tsunami swept over your town, many of your family and friends were killed and your community was devastated.

How bleak is that? Now if ever there were cause for depression, this would be it! What could anybody do to console you? Would this awful tragedy at such a young age leave you trapped in a deep depression for the rest of your life? How could you possibly recover? What impact would such earth shattering circumstances have on your religious life and your spiritual beliefs? How would these beliefs aid in the recovery of your mental health amidst such devastation?

OK, this may be a very extreme example, but I bring it up for an important reason. The truth is, every month and every year people do survive and recover from tragedies such as this throughout the world. They even overcome these seemingly insurmountable troubles without the benefit of ECT or any other therapy for that matter. How do they do it? All it really takes is time and will for things to get better if one appropriately allows the normal occurrence of processing feelings to take place. With ECT, people are taught that all of us have the power to overcome almost any loss or devastation that life may throw at us.

Time and therapy are an incredibly powerful combination. Of course, it requires trust on the part of the client, and both client and therapist must view themselves as partners in the therapy process. This in turn gives power to the client. How better to give power to the client than have the client become their own therapist?

There is, however, one big obstacle that too often gets in the way – before the process can even begin. It is very common for people to spend lots of energy running away from debilitating feelings of fear and grief. Teenagers do this every bit as much as adults – but in both cases they are running in the exact opposite direction. In ECT, the goal is not to avoid our feelings, but to learn from them. For example, a very talented teenager twists her ankle doing a back flip in gymnastics practice. She is so traumatized by the pain that she is shaken to the core with fear and decides to quit the gymnastics team. Think how much better off this girl would be if she analyzed her feelings rather than attempting to bury them. Instead of hanging up her shoes and ending her career, she could ask her coach, "How did I land improperly? What caused the injury? What can I do to prevent it from happening again?" If she had learned Emotional Core Therapy, she would have understood how to respect her authentic feelings of fear, and then release it by discovering how to improve her technique, rather than quitting the sport.

How can she do this (respect her authentic feelings)? By learning how to monitor her own body and the signals that it is constantly providing to her. This is one of the keys to successfully using ECT, and it works for all kinds of situations in life. The releasing of feelings can involve any loss in life, or any fearful event. Since we are all unique, none of us will release our feelings in the exact same way. It's a bit of a discovery process. For example, there was a fifteen-year old boy named Justin who was having difficulty with some of his classes. Nothing seemed to help, until one day some new neighbors moved in next door. They had a boy the same age and the two soon became friends. It turned out that this kid had some of the same problems in school as Justin. They would have long conversations, and soon things began to improve for Justin. Why? The reason is because they shared something in common and just talking with this new friend helped Justin to release his feelings. The point is, releasing feelings is a very natural process, and often takes place in unexpected places and usually unintentionally. It does not by any means always have to take place in a therapist's office.

Another example could involve a young, shy 17-year old male. He falls head over heels for a girl at his high school. Sadly, after three months of intense dating, she abruptly breaks up with him. Emotionally devastated, he withdraws into a shell and stops dating altogether. Now ask yourself, would it have been much more emotionally healthy for this young man to instead honor his pain of grief/loss? I believe yes! Rather than stop dating, he needs to accept the experience and view it as part of a learning process. Easy? No, not by a long shot. It takes time (often months and even years) to understand one's feelings, which is why it is a continual learning process to learn ECT. But the benefits are real and often life-changing!

As these examples illustrate, we can learn a lot by examining a combination of various real life and hypothetical scenarios of people just like you struggling with the stresses of life, which is precisely the approach of the rest of this book. The goal is to help teens learn how to cope effectively with debilitating feelings. One of the primary purposes of this book is to demonstrate several psychological techniques in a fun and relaxed manner. It is always comforting and help-ful to know that others have gone through, and continue to experience, the very same kinds of situations that you do.

At its core, ECT involves externalizing one's feelings rather than internalizing them. There is a time and a place for releasing feelings, and common sense must be used. What we are trying to do is to get our feelings outside of us, and this is a process that takes time, like learning to ride a bike or to swim. For example, imagine if you found out that one of your friends, jealous of your athletic abilities, told your coach a big lie about you that got you kicked off the basket-ball team. Do you think that you would just bounce back from something like that overnight? Of course not! The feelings of anger and loss would be all too genuine, and prop-erly releasing them would not come quickly. On the other hand, however, it would be quite regrettable to put this off too long, which would be very unhealthy for both your mind and body. Toxic beliefs, if internalized, can cause unneces-sary stress and damage to the body. This in turn leads to body function problems such as muscle tightness, hand sweating and trembling. Don't underestimate the seriousness of this. A person who is under stress all of the time is risking damage to their organs, which is of course extremely hazardous.

Imagine the situation of a junior in high school named Megan. She comes to therapy because she finds that she is in a depressed state. Megan is suffering from major states of depression such as agitation, bad mood, no joy, oversleeping, lack of energy, and feeling useless. Both of her parents work so many hours that they can't give her much attention, and she is an only child. To make things worse, Megan had caught her best friend sneaking around with her boyfriend behind her back. At first she forgave him – but then he did the same thing with another girl. This time their break-up was permanent.

When Megan first begins therapy her level of depression is about an eight or nine (on a scale of one to ten). If she was already under a psychiatric doctor's care for depression, chances are good that the prescription medications she would be on might take the edge off her feelings, but they still would not lift her out of her funk. When Megan complains of being "unloved, unwanted, lonely, sad, tired," and crying a great deal, it will not be difficult for her therapist to assess her problem as too much grief or loss. Too much grief or loss is another name for depression. Megan is also suffering several bodily symptoms including lack of sleep, trouble eating and feeling fatigued.

Megan has belonged to the Lutheran church her entire life, but when the depression started becoming really painful, she felt too overwhelmed to turn to God to help deal with her pain. Using Emotional Core Therapy, together she and her therapist would start to reframe some of her thinking, including showing her how much of a profound impact her faith could have on her recovery if only she were provided the right tools. Moreover, she will start to recognize that most of her thoughts are due to leaving a long-term relationship. Her overwhelming feelings of psychic pain will begin to lessen over time as she learns to isolate the problem. As she becomes more and more aware of the four authentic feelings, she is going to recognize that she has too much grief in her life. Over the course of eight to ten months, she will begin to release her feelings both in therapy and in her daily life.

Emotional Core Therapy will teach Megan that another way to combat her depression is by working to bring more joy into her life. For example, her therapist would probably urge her to make a list of twenty attributes that she likes about herself. As they discuss the list of twenty joyful characteristics, they will see if a main theme continues to pop up. For example, let's say Megan has a wonderful and truly loving relationship with her grandparents. They live across town but whenever she can she takes the bus and visits them, and they are always so happy to see her. Using this information, Megan's therapist would highlight how she was able to bring joy to her grandparents' life, and in turn to her own.

As a Lutheran, Megan had known since she was a young child that reading the Bible is a key to feeling the love of God. Even the simple saying she'd learned as a little girl when she first started going to Bible school emphasized this: "Jesus loves me, this I know, because my Bible tells me so." Reading the gospels, in particular the Gospel according to John with all of its emphasis on the love of God for all of humanity, brought a joy to Megan's heart that she had forgot even existed.

Megan wasn't trying to become a Bible scholar, or impress people at church with all of the extra Bible reading that had now become a part of her life. Instead, she was simply letting the joy that seemed to flow off of those pages into her mind and her heart. Like ECT, it helped put things into their proper perspective. Another scripture she came across in her reading, from the book of Romans, brought a great deal of assurance to her whenever she began to feel isolated or unloved. It was the passage where Paul explains: "For I am convinced that neither death, nor life, nor angels, nor principalities, nor things present, nor things to come, nor powers, nor height, nor depth, nor any other created thing, will be able to **separate us from the love of God**, which is in Christ Jesus our Lord."

When Megan prayed, she would let her mind wander and sometimes daydream. With her focus on Christ, simple thoughts not requiring too much cognition, her prayers not only honored God, but they served as a form of meditation that helped to slow down Megan's central nervous system. As she was learning more about Emotional Core Therapy, she knew that this was precisely the goal of step eight of ECT. In fact, she came to realize that the entire process was a splendid combination of religion and psychology that really made sense to her. Megan felt deep in her heart that Jesus had led her to ECT, as it had the effect of strengthening her faith while at the same time bringing peace to her mind and to her soul.

As part of using ECT, Megan would also start to do other things that bring her joy herself. For example, power walking for exercise and stress reduction, along with making new friends who are much more respectful of her needs. This will help Megan to reduce her level of depression from a seven or eight level to a three to five level over the course of her therapy.

Now let's take a look at Megan's relationship stress utilizing the eight step ECT Flowchart. An important reminder to all teenagers is that aspects of these eight steps happen whenever one experiences stress. From the time you are a baby in diapers, the four emotions are going to be with you. These four emotions when severe enough, will cause you bodily stress till your last day on earth. What could be more important than learning how to effectively cope with these emotions?

For step one of the ECT process, Megan was entering a new relationship with self, other people, places, or things. In this case, Megan was in a relationship with her boyfriend for an extended period of time. As ECT mentions, when it comes to relationships, when they come together or grow apart from us, we experience stress.

In step two of the ECT process, Megan was understanding that the needs of relationships are what cause her stress.

We break these needs down into four categories. Emotional, financial, spiritual, and physical. In her relationship with her boyfriend, Megan experienced all four of these emotions daily. It is important to remember that sometimes we only experience one or two of these needs. Every relationship encounter varies in the needs required for that relationship.

In step three of the ECT process, Megan utilized her five senses to perceive the needs of her boyfriend. These senses are hearing, touching, smelling, tasting and seeing. For Megan, she heard and saw her boyfriend acting in an unfaithful and dishonest manner. This step happens almost automatically for nearly all teens.

In step four of the ECT process, Megan experienced the authentic feeling of grief when the relationship ended. Earlier in the relationship Megan had lots of fun/joy with her boyfriend. Now that he was no longer in her life, she had lots of sadness/grief because she missed his companionship.

In step five of the ECT process, Megan's emotions traveled throughout her central nervous system. From her brain throughout the muscles, tendons, and ligaments in her body. Megan, like nearly all humans, experienced this step automatically.

In step six of the ECT process, Megan experienced uncomfortable bodily stress and tension such as agitation, oversleeping, lack of energy, and a bad mood.

In step seven of the ECT process, Megan learned to release this bodily stress. She did this by verbalizing her emotions with a counselor, praying, power walking and exercise, as a way to release her stress.

In step eight of the ECT process, Megan practiced daily meditation exercises to balance her equilibrium and quiet her mind. Prayer was an integral way that Megan and her family used to relax and self soothe themselves while maintaining and strengthening her faith in God. Megan strengthened her relationship with Jesus through this stressful encounter with her boyfriend. She realized that Jesus is with her hourly and daily and she can rely on Him when needed.

As we go through each new case in this spiritual book for teens, try and visualize each step the character will encounter. As you feel more mastery of the eight step process, try and discover how each step of the ECT process is involved in your own relationships at home, school, or with friends.

If Megan drops in for a visit to her therapist a few years later, in all probability she will look much better. She may well be a senior in college engaged to a great guy whom she truly loves. Emotional Core Therapy can't promise such results – nothing can – but it can definitely offer a teen like Megan hope that she might otherwise never have.

Prescription medications alone are unlikely to be as effective as ECT. They might numb Megan's pain but they would do little to change her underlying condition of a poor relationship. Her therapist would work with her to decrease her medication until eventually she doesn't need them at all. This will allow Megan the opportunity to reduce her self-described addiction to prescription drugs and begin to change her life for the better.

Many people try to self-medicate in a number of different ways, including teenagers. Some like to lose themselves in partying, while others choose to rebel against their parents. They are using these things as a way of trying to avoid loss or grief. What they fail to recognize, however, is that these feelings are a natural and normal part of life. When using Emotional Core Therapy to treat depression, you will learn the proper coping mechanisms for processing grief. The time varies from person to person and from one situation to another. The severity of the situation makes a big difference. Losing a five-dollar bill is not going to cause as much as grief as finding out that you have cancer. The real problem with drowning your pain away or numbing yourself is that it does not work. It only delays the inevitable: at some point you have to fully grieve the loss.

Emotional Core Therapy teaches us to calm the body by staying in a peaceful, meditative state throughout the day. By remaining this way for a prolonged period you can identify all fearful and toxic events in your life. This includes drugs or alcohol. A person that understands how a hot stove works would not touch it because they understand that it causes burns and pain. The same can be said for drugs and alcohol. Why would you use something that could cause legal and financial trouble? Why would you use something that could cause so much damage to your body or even kill you?

Do the research! Go on the Net and find out for yourself. The more information one has about illicit drugs or alcohol, the less likely they will be to use them. Would someone really want to use methamphetamine (also known as "speed"), for example, if they knew the harm that it could cause to their body, or heroin, if they fully understood that an overdose could kill them? As if that weren't bad enough, with illegal drugs nobody knows exactly what is in it, meaning it often includes toxic substances that can be deadly. You may need to notify your medical doctor when you have serious mental health problems, but especially problems with addictions. Medical doctors have a good understanding of these issues and how to address them.

Oftentimes young people seek out legal or illegal drugs, alcohol, or prescription drugs to numb the emotional pain of fear or grief. But rarely, if ever, does this work to treat the underlying issue. You have to change the relationship issue that is causing you emotional trauma to fix relationship problems. Let's look at a high school tennis player for an example. When he begins his serve, he twists his back a certain way every time, because of poor technique. Every day, he comes home and takes a pain reliever for his shoulder and back pain. The medication will not change his poor technique that is causing the problem in the first place. This young tennis player needs a coach to teach him a proper serve with less torque so he won't twist his back out every time. By changing his behavior (poor swing) the boy learns a proper swing and won't have to take medications continuously. Besides, medications, drugs, and alcohol, usually have side effects which can hurt your performance in tennis matches. Ever see a tennis player with a headache and a hangover play! Not a pretty sight!

Now let's look at a real life situation. A high school freshman girl enters her math class. She gets a grouchy old man, near retirement, as her teacher. The old man is mean to all the kids. He yells and gives detentions out all the time. It is a legal form of abuse. The young girl sees her high school counselor who in turn refers her to a psychiatrist who prescribes her medication to relax. What is wrong with this picture? Why not change the relationship that is causing this stress in the first place? Get a new teacher! Switch schools! Complain to the principal, etc. The point is, if the young girl can change her relationship with the teacher, she won't need to take medications or drugs for months or years. She can honor her authentic feelings of fear and work towards a result that will release those feelings. Better yet, when she is a senior, and she is assigned "a mean old hag" as a chemistry teacher, she will know how to assert herself. Not only that, but when her new boyfriend causes her fear by teasing her in front of her friends, she will know exactly what to do! Why? The techniques of ECT are easy to learn and can be transferred from situation to situation. They provide your life with a sense of power and vitality that you will never experience if you lose yourself in a haze of drugs and alcohol.

Consider a scenario of someone who decides to smoke pot every day to cope. What happens? She may get suspended.

Miss valuable school time. Get in trouble with the police. Hurt her chances for acceptance to a good college. Not to mention she will have to deal with the side effects of marijuana like fatigue and lack of energy. Probably not a smart way to try to cope.

ECT, by stark contrast, offers a genuine way to cope with problems, and it can also help with addictions (both kicking them and never developing them in the first place). Since addictive tendencies often begin during the teen years it's very important for you to learn how properly releasing your authentic feelings can help you to avoid all kinds of big problems down the road.

Addiction is described as follows: Compulsive physiological and psychological need for a habit-forming substance. **The condition of being habitually or compulsively occupied with or in something. For example, someone having an addiction to shopping or fast cars.**

Here is a list of some of the most common addictions (it does not include the abuse of narcotics, as it is a list of legal addictions, but the use of illegal drugs of course can lead to serious and even fatal addictions for lots of individuals, including young people).

10. Shopping

Compulsive shopping may sound funny, but it's very serious and can have disastrous consequences for your finances.

9. TV

It's hard to experience real life when you spend half the day plunked in front of the TV. Your teenage years are a great time to learn about the world – by actually experiencing it.

8. Video Games

The video game world is also not real life. Sure, it can be a fun way to spend time. But if you spend too much time on video games, they can indeed become quite addictive, keeping you away from more important and productive things.

7. Celebrity Gossip

Everybody likes to read stories about celebs, all the "who is dating who" stuff and the latest "dirt." But why get so caught up in the lives of celebrities? These aren't people that you know in your real life. Try to take only a passing interest in that stuff. Your time is too valuable for much more than that.

6. Fast Food

Yes, it's cheap and it tastes good. But you also know how unhealthy fast food is. If you get addicted to it as a teen, these cravings could become a habit for life – which is definitely something that you want to avoid.

5. Gambling

You may not be old enough to go to a casino yet, but lots of teenagers get caught up with gambling in a number of different ways, often involving sports. Bad idea. It almost always ends up losing money and can later develop into a very serious bad habit as an adult. Avoid it now rather than regret it later.

4. Pornography

OK, maybe it seems harmless at first. After all, you are at an age where thinking about sexual topics is completely normal and natural. So is being curious. But pornography is such an unhealthy way to explore one's sexuality. It objectifies human beings and conjures up misleading ideas about sex and love, and ultimately leads to addiction for many people. At that point, it is no longer harmless in any way.

3. Alcohol

First, if you are under 21 it is illegal for you to drink alcohol anywhere in the United States. Moreover, once a person starts drinking, it can be extremely difficult to stop and not get sucked in by this powerful addiction. Think of how many people are killed and maimed by drunk drivers every year. Not to mention what alcohol does to your liver and your brain. The last thing you want is to become yet another statistic.

2. Cigarettes

In recent years, the government and society at large have been trying to warn people about the dangers of tobacco. Like alcohol, once you start it can be incredibly hard to stop. Cigarettes contain nicotine, which is highly addictive. Spare yourself from an early grave and never pick up this bad habit in the first place.

1. Prescription Drugs

At different times in our lives, we may need to take prescription drugs for very legitimate reasons. For example, you may have been injured playing sports and your doctor prescribed painkillers. The problem with these drugs is people can easily become dependent on them. Don't think that it can't happen to you! Other people, both your age and older, thought the same thing but soon ended up with a serious addiction crisis in their life. Use extreme caution even with drugs that are prescribed to you – and never use a drug that is not prescribed to you. That could land you either in jail or with serious health issues.

Getting back specifically to ECT's treatment of depression, it can be very creative in the ways that it supports patients. For example, young man I talked to remembered the words of Bruce Springsteen's hit, "Born in the USA," a song about the troubled life of a returning Vietnam War veteran. We talked about that song, and sometimes we even play songs in therapy as a tool. There is something comforting about the song's powerful music and defiant lyrics, which seem determined to overcome all of the hardship. It helps relieve some of the grief to talk about whatever it is that hurts us, and it's a great way to help release feelings.

One of the reasons that music is such an excellent technique to release feelings is the sheer magnitude of songs. It could be Hard Rock, Rap, Pop, Country, you name it some artist has recorded a song for nearly every possible type of relationship issue or problem. All four authentic feelings have hundreds, if not thousands of songs that people can relate to in every culture and virtually every personal situation.

Another tool might be to talk about movies. Consider "Titanic" for example. It's a story of young love cut tragically short by one of the most famous disasters of the twentieth century. When a viewer watches this type of film it is possible to evoke some hidden feelings of loss. This kind of reading of toxic feelings happens to most of us daily in some fashion when we maybe watch some of the soaps on TV or listen to a sad song on your IPod. None of this is meant to be morbid. The point is, hiding from grief does not make it go away and it does not cure depression. To the contrary, identifying the feelings of loss, is the first step in coping with those feelings, and sometimes things like songs and movies can help us put our finger on the problem spot.

The one common factor in each of the examples we are discussing is that they are all about loss. But simply knowing that is not enough. We need to explore deeper, to get to the roots of what these relationships were truly about.

Another client, Austin, was dealing with a different set of circumstances. He did not have a great voice in his family, and consequently never really had anyone to confide in. His father was a hard driving workaholic, so Austin worked hard too. He took a job washing dishes in the kitchen of a nursing home, spent a lot of night hours at work, and didn't have many friends (and the few he did seemed to always be out having fun while he was working). Worse yet for Austin, his family lived in a secluded subdivision that did not have many young people living nearby. So his issue coming to therapy was isolation and despair, which are terms otherwise known as loss or grief.

A few years earlier, Austin had developed an interest in Zen Buddhism. But Austin had fallen away from these beliefs until he began ECT. Then he remembered something he'd read in a book about the Korean Zen master Seung Sahn. This wise sage would always instruct his students to not cling to their fixed ideas about the world and about people. Austin realized that ECT could help him to rid himself of this "clinginess" and replace with it something far healthier.

Using the authentic nature of ECT, I was able to show Austin how his feelings of grief were connected to his lack of friends and support. In therapy, I was able to draw a small picture of how the four authentic feelings work and Austin was able to see that his powerful feelings of sadness were situational to his job, where he lived, and spending so much time away from friends. When Austin began counseling with my office he was near a nine on the one to ten-point scale of sadness ratings. This was however a temporary state. We discussed Austin's early childhood where he was often very happy playing ice hockey with his friends. He was able to see his feelings of grief were tied to entering a new relationship (in a new job isolated from people his own age)

As part of our therapy, Austin made a list of ten things that would bring him joy. His top five wishes were better grades, a scholarship for college, a new car, a new girlfriend, and more time with his friends. Over the course of the next 14 months, Austin began to work towards those five dreams that would bring him joy. He was able to achieve two to three of his desired ways to bring joy into his life. His level of grief plummeted from an eight or nine to two to four as Austin began to feel more supported and loved in his life.

Austin also began to see the world around him differently the more he continued to study Buddhism and incorporate its teachings into what he was learning through ECT. For example, the Four Noble Truths of Buddhism:

1. Suffering is part of life.
2. Suffering comes from attachments.
3. Cessation of suffering is attainable.
4. There is a clear path we can take to the cessation of suffering.

Austin was especially encouraged by the belief that an ending of suffering is indeed attainable. This belief lifted up Austin's spirits whenever he started feeling down. He acknowledged that suffering is a part of life, but so is healing. Emotional Core Therapy reinforced this concept for Austin, because it too, in a very open and up front manner, assured him that his concerns and feelings were perfectly normal, but, they did not have to overwhelm him and make him feel like these negative thoughts would go on forever. With the right frame of mind, and an understanding of how to process his emotions in a healthy way, Austin gradually became more optimistic about the future.

In therapy, he was honest about his feelings. He genuinely wanted to get better. One of the first big decisions he made was to ask his boss to cut back his hours working in the kitchen at the nursing home. His boss agreed, and Austin soon started spending more time with his friends on nights and weekends, sometimes just hanging out, other times playing hockey with them. This made him feel more connected not only to other kids his own age, but to life itself. You see, it was important for Austin to build a support network so that he would not feel so isolated.

Emotional Core Therapy uses various techniques to help people help themselves to get better. In this case, we helped Austin to recognize what he wanted out of life. He wanted a girlfriend, a new car, and some relaxation doing fun stuff with friends. At the time, he had none of these things, but he recognized that he could work for them and – most critically – he had the power to get them.

The ECT therapist is like a cheerleader: very supportive of the patient. They go at their own speed and of their own volition. It wasn't the therapist's role to tell Austin what to do. He, like every patient, has to work that out on his own. The therapist is there to support him, trying different things, to assist him in his journey to recovery.

The therapist helps the patient to not be fearful about obtaining what they want from life. Don't let anyone ever tell you that you are too young to know these things about yourself. After all, it is *your* life, and whatever your age, you are the only one who can live it. In ECT, we talk about basic feelings so if there is something that you are afraid of, we want to explore that. We teach people to be respectful of themselves and to acknowledge that they are indeed worthy of working everything out. No, it doesn't come overnight. For example, in Austin's situation he was able to achieve two of his goals, but not all of them – at least not initially. But what really matters is that he was able to bring joy into his life. That was missing when all of his focus was on his depression and he felt utterly powerless to do anything about it.

Next, let's take a look at a hypothetical case involving a Muslim girl named Farid, a high school student who loves spending time with her friends every chance she gets. The time that she spends with them both during and after school are at the center of her social life. That is when she talks with her friends about anything and everything, and she truly relishes those special moments.

But then something quite unexpected happens. Her father gets a new job in another state and the family has to relocate. For Farid it is devastating. Being uprooted like this it feels like her life was ruined. She keeps in touch with her friends by phone and text, but it just isn't the same. She really cares about those kids, and losing them is more than just a major bummer – it causes her tremendous grief.

Using ECT, a therapist would help show Farid how to process that grief. As part of her healing, Farid would come to embrace her religion even more fully than she had before. However, even though her parents can help her with religious instruction, they don't have the training to help her with ECT, and she therefore needs outside assistance. ECT would allow her to tell the stories of her pain and to process her feelings in ways that are healthy and promote mental healing. She could also identify and label her authentic feelings of grief in therapy. These kinds of ECT sessions would likely be filled with crying and feeling angry with her parents for moving so far away from the only home she had ever known. She can no longer spend hour upon hour with her friends going to the mall and doing gymnastics and other fun stuff together. This is something that she must come to accept. Farid would learn that there is no magic cure or pill for grief. It is a necessary part of life. We can only learn from the pain and become better individuals in the future.

In Farid's case, she needs to make new friends at her new school and new neighborhood. As she and her family are Islamic, one of the first places she is able to make new connections with other girls her age is at the local mosque, which fortunately is very close to her new home. She probably does not want to be a "loner" just because she is the new girl. ECT would show her that all of the good qualities that made her friends back in her home state (who were still her friends, albeit at a long distance) like her in the first place, would appeal to kids in this new place as well.

During this transition, she also recalled the translated meaning of her name: Farid means "unique." She decided to utilize the connotation of that beautiful word as part of her therapy. Farid reflected on the fact that she is a unique creation of Allah. Her religion taught her that as a unique human being, she has something to offer the new people who were now coming into her life. And they had something to offer her too, for the girls she met at the mosque not only shared the same faith, they also held similar interests in food, sports, movies and many other things. She soon started to not feel so alone – and depressed – anymore.

ECT also greatly helped Farid by making her prayer life not only more honoring to Allah, but also more beneficial to her as a worshiper. In her mind she visualized the Black Stone, which is the eastern cornerstone of the Kaaba, the ancient stone building located in the center of the Grand Mosque in Mecca, Saudi Arabia. Considered sacred by Muslims, Farid hoped to visit it someday when she would go there on a pilgrimage, which all Muslims aspire to do at least once during their lifetime.

Such imagery had a calming effect on Farid, and she knew that, just as is the goal of step eight of ECT, it was slowing down her central nervous system. Indeed, she could literally *feel* this happening every day, which was a very welcome development. Farid was gradually becoming more adept at noticing how each of the eight steps of ECT integrated so well into her life. As a person with strong religious convictions, ECT seemed to be bridging the gap between psychology and spirituality. The more she learned about her mind and how it works and how to keep it healthy, the more she understood how her faith could be an integral part of her recovery.

In addition to lifting up and transforming her prayer life, using and processing authentic feelings of joy and grief in therapy, ECT would show Farid the importance of building up her new support network of friends where she now lived. She would be able to learn from her debilitating feelings of sadness and have more hope for the future. Just as our aspiring gymnast in an earlier example was better off learning from her painful ankle injury, Farid would in turn be better off for processing and identifying her four authentic feelings of joy, grief, fear, and relief. She needs to be determined to make better decisions about when and where to make friends.

Oftentimes clients like Farid need a hug, tissue, and a non-judgmental atmosphere to release their foreign feelings of sadness. If Farid is a visual learner, she and her therapist would be able to diagram her supportive relationships and identify and isolate her feelings of loss. Both the visual and verbal means of expression would allow Farid to release her sadness over a period of a few months. The goal would be to help her work towards making new friends, without giving up her old friends, so that she could strike the proper balance in her life.

By making friends in an atmosphere where she felt safe and nurtured, amongst a strong faith-based community, Farid knew that she was taking steps toward leaving her past behind by learning to enjoy rather than dread her new circumstances. Islam teaches people to submit their own will to the will of Allah, which really helped build up Farid's confidence that in the long run, if she both remained faithful to her religion, and continued following ECT's gentle suggestions, her problems would inevitably become manageable.

One option might be for Farid to begin to take (acoustic) guitar lessons to regain her sense of calm and peace. By strumming soft songs, she would be able to begin her process of self-care and self-soothing. Of course, it is important to again reiterate that what works for one client as a form of relaxation may not work for another. Farid mind needs to be allowed to daydream and relax through an activity such as playing the guitar. Other people may find learning to play a musical instrument a chore and mentally taxing. The exact form of relaxation that you choose isn't what really matters. It does matter, however, that you discover the best way for you as an individual to relax. This is an important step in Emotional Core Therapy, as it allows the mind a way to daydream and flow freely.

Let's now examine Farid's stressful relocation to another home and school using the Eight Step ECT flowchart. In step one of the ECT process we examine that the entering and leaving of relationships is what causes teens stress. This can be the relationship you have with yourself, another human being, a place or thing. In this case, by moving to another state as her permanent residence, Farid was leaving many valued relationships. She was also entering into many new relationships in her new surroundings.

In step two of the ECT process, Farid realized that leaving loving relationships meant that new stress would occur because her emotional, financial, spiritual and physical needs would be changing and lessening with her old friends. Her new home also meant new needs would have to be addressed. One of the new demands upon her which turned out well was making new friends at her new mosque.

In step three of the ECT process Farid learned that her five senses perceived these needs, which stressed her out in an uncomfortable manner. All five of her senses (hearing, touching, smelling, tasting and seeing) were used almost automatically by Farid to examine the needs of others.

In step four of the ECT process, Farid experienced all four of the four true emotions intensely during the moving process. The predominant feeling was grief for a period of time as she had diminished contact with close friends. As she made new friends at her mosque, she began to experience more joy in her life.

In step five of the ECT process, Farid's emotional duress sent messages throughout her central nervous system. This includes her brain and muscles in her body. This step happened quite automatically for Farid as it does for all humans.

In step six of the ECT process, Farid experienced some uncomfortable bodily stress because of her family relocating. This included feeling angry and crying.

In step seven of the ECT process Farid learned to discharge those disrupting emotions. Farid used prayer, and verbalization of her emotions to release stress. She also diagramed her relationship pain and by putting it on a piece of paper, validated her pain. She also played the guitar to release her sadness/grief.

Lastly, since Farid was a practicing Muslim, she dutifully prayed throughout the day. This was a great way for her to daily meditate. As we mentioned previously, simple quiet prayer can be incorporated into ECT as the eighth and final step. The key in using prayer as a form of meditation is to slow down the central nervous system. This can occur if we don't use a great deal of cognition/ thought, and allow our mind to wander, free float, and daydream in a relaxed manner.

Another hypothetical case involves an aspiring teen writer named Abby who dreams of being famous writer like her father. She had attended writing seminars during her first two summers in high school, took AP literature and hired a tutor to help improve her grades even further. Abby had even quit the swim team so she could stay after school and write short stories for her school newspaper.

Abby has always considered herself a secular person. It's not that she has ever been hostile to religion or to other people's beliefs. To the contrary, she found them fascinating, and had even made it a goal that as she grew older she might learn more about such things. As a writer, she was also an avid reader, and she was familiar with teachings such as "love thy neighbour" from the Christian Bible and the words of wisdom from religious figures such as the Dalai Lama. But the beliefs and practices of these religions were not a part of daily life or her belief system.

Here's some good news about that: when it comes to ECT, a perspective such as Abby's is perfectly OK. ECT does not require a person to have any kind of religious faith at all, and is never judgemental against anyone for what they either believe or do not believe.

The important thing for people who do have religious faith to remember is, your faith should never be dependent on some other person's perspective on things. Learn to agree to disagree. So what if you see the world differently than how some other person sees it? ECT takes the approach that diversity of opinion when it comes to matters of faith is simply a reflection of the diversity that makes human beings and life in general so interesting. Indeed, it is what makes each one of us sacred. Those who believe in the Creator believe that He gave every one of us our individuality in His image. Regardless of whether you believe that or not, ECT will be equally effective for you because one thing that we can certainly all agree upon is that we are all human. And that is the only requirement for getting started with ECT.

Now, back to Abby. The summer before her senior year, she applies to four of the best writing colleges on the East Coast. She is crushed by disappointment when all four reject her application. During her senior year, Abby often finds herself crying uncontrollably. She has trouble sleeping and eating and can barely concentrate in class. Her grades go into a free fall and she starts getting into arguments with her boyfriend.

What is really happening to Abby? She is suffering from excessive grief. This scenario could happen to most anyone in high school. How do we help someone in Abby's situation using Emotional Core Therapy? With ECT we would focus on authentic feelings of joy grief, fear, and relief. We would spend a good amount of time helping Abby cathartically release those toxic feelings of loss/grief, and spend some time helping her find joy in her life. This would include making a list of 20 things that bring her joy. Abby and her therapist would set a goal of trying to initially obtain at least four or five of these. The list would likely include simple things such as a day at a spa, getting ice cream, going to the movies, a day at the beach, etc.

Using ECT, Abby would also learn some loving yourself meditative techniques like taking a Jacuzzi, walking the dog, and many others. We would educate Abby on the definition of loving yourself and teach her the eight-step ECT process.

Later on in Abby's life, once she has committed ECT to her long-term memory, she will be able to transfer what she has learned to other situations/relationships. When her boyfriend breaks up with her she will suffer grief. When her grandmother gets sick and passes on, Abby will grieve. The difference is as an adult, she will learn much quicker how to identify and process the four authentic feelings of joy, grief, fear and relief. This will greatly improve her quality of life, and make it less likely that she will suffer from long bouts of severe depression.

One other case that demonstrates ECT's effectiveness in treating depression involved a young man named Ryan, an eighteen-year-old recent high school graduate. Ryan had a girlfriend that he loved and adored. He worked for the family business, and the idea had been that he was supposed to make a lot of money following in his father's footsteps. But his father whom he worked for was very demanding. Moreover, the young man worked inside an office building all day, which he didn't really like at all.

In ECT therapy, we let him talk out his feelings. He shared things about himself, such as that when he was in high school he was a very good athlete. He also had a strong Christian faith and he had been attending the same Baptist church in his neighborhood since he was a little boy. He was able to recognize and identify the things in life that brought him joy. These included working closely with people; he actually preferred to be working outside, not inside. As a matter of fact, he found great satisfaction working with his hands, rather than sitting at a desk all day.

Ryan could not shake his depression until he changed several of his relationships that were causing him grief. He was sad that he had to work underneath a demanding and mean spirited father. Ryan was also sad that he had to work an isolated job as an office worker, which meant he had to work indoors all day even when it was sunny and beautiful outside.

When Ryan came to see me his level of sadness/depression was at an eight or nine! Fortunately for Ryan, he had the time and determination to alter his relationships that were causing him grief.

We also discussed Ryan's faith. One of the key tenets of Bible-based Christianity is that Jesus Christ leads us to the Father. Yes, as the Ten Commandments require, Ryan would continue to honor his earthly father. But he soon realized that when it came to his own life and his own independence, he had to do what was right for himself—and turning to his Father in heaven helped him to make that important decision.

ECT guided Ryan in understanding his feelings, but when he combined that newly acquired understanding with his faith in God's provision for his life – something his church had always emphasized – it all began to make sense on a spiritual level as well as intellectually. Ryan was now fully engaging both his heart and his mind, and his entire being reaped the benefits of this new, liberating and incredibly honest approach to dealing with his ow feelings. It was truly unlike anything else he had ever experienced before.

When Ryan would pray to Jesus, he didn't follow any specific formula. Instead, his prayers were very simple and always supremely peaceful. This helped him maintain a tranquil state of mind, which had the very beneficial effect of calming his central nervous system, precisely as we do in step eight of ECT.

Over the course of twelve months, he was able to quit his job and go to a vocational school where he started training for a job with a major utility company. Ryan came back to visit me a year after therapy ended to report that he had proudly earned employee of the month at his new, much happier job. His level of depression dropped from a nine to a one or two in just over a year.

Of course, no two people experience depression in the exact same way or for the exact same reasons. Therefore, we always need to treat people as individuals with unique problems and solutions that depend upon their own particular circumstances. However, Emotional Core Therapy offers solutions based on abilities that all of us innately possess. The therapy is successful because it works *with* your emotions rather than treating them as some kind of enemy or outsider. Depression and sadness, after all, are natural aspects of life, but the sooner and more precisely we understand what brings them about, the closer we are to moving on to a happier and more peaceful frame of mind.

List Five Relationships That You Have Exited That Have Brought You "Grief"

A) MOVING OUT OF STATE

B) FAILING A CLASS AT SCHOOL

1.

2.

3.

4.

5.

Notes:

List Five Ways You Can Release Feelings Of Grief

A) JOURNALING

B) SINGING

1.

2.

3.

4.

5.

SYMPTOMS OF DEPRESSION

CRYING SPELLS FOR NO APPARENT REASON

LOSS OF INTEREST OR PLEASURE IN NORMAL ACTIVITIES

CHANGES IN APPETITE

FATIGUE, TIREDNESS AND LOSS OF ENERGY

FEELINGS OF SADNESS OR UNHAPPINESS

IRRITABILITY OR FRUSTRATION, EVEN OVER SMALL MATTERS

INDECISIVENESS, DISTRACTIBILITY AND DECREASED CONCENTRATION

List Five Of Your Own Symptoms Of Depression

1.

2.

3.

4.

5.

Notes:

ECT Flow Chart

Relationships;
self, other people, places, things

⬇

Needs;
emotional, financial, spiritual, physical

⬇

Five Senses;
seeing, touching, smelling, tasting, hearing

⬇

Four Authentic Feelings;
joy, grief, fear, relief

⬇

Effects;
brain/central nervous system

⬇

Uncomfortable Symptoms;
muscle tightness, fatigue, etc.

⬇

Releasing Process;
learn to discharge toxic feelings

⬇

Balancing Your Equilibrium;
practice various daily meditative techniques

CHAPTER THREE
Using ECT to Treat Anxiety

This chapter on anxiety will build on what you have already learned about Emotional Core Therapy. We will again use a variety of mostly fictional situations to illustrate how ECT helps you to live a better life and to solve problems with as little fear as possible.

Before going any further, let's ask a very simple question: what exactly is this debilitating feeling of "fear"? The simplest definition is that it is really just another word for "anxiety." As we discussed in the beginning of this book, it is entering a relationship that you dislike that causes fear. A good example of someone entering a relationship they dislike would be a child or a teenager living in a country torn by warfare. You have seen video on TV of what conditions are like in places such as Iraq and Afghanistan. Close your eyes and try to imagine that you lived under those circumstances, never knowing when a bomb might go off or gunfire could suddenly erupt. Any normal human being (of any age) would be fearful or afraid. In other words, your "relationship" with the war would make you experience fear. All of the cases in this chapter, though not nearly as extreme as warfare, will examine characters entering relationships that they dislike. You will see how ECT can potentially help in each of these situations.

The first example that we use involves a nineteen-year old named Drew. He came to my office complaining of feeling scared about his life. He was nervous that he was not his usual self. He was terrified that he was not living up to being a man. He joined the military, but once he got to boot camp he had a difficult time fulfilling the rigorous requirements and ultimately dropped out. Drew became worried about his self-esteem, and he felt weak for not being able to successfully complete boot camp. The experience was very demanding on the young recruit. The drill instructor was mean spirited, hostile and angry all day long. Drew would wake up at the crack of dawn with the drill instructor yelling at him. He would then be ordered around all day and night by this very demanding guy. Drew was pushed to his limits both physically and mentally during his thirty-day ordeal that included shooting guns off, sleep-deprivation, hot sun, and severe weather conditions.

When we examine some of the feelings that Drew faced we see that he used words such as terrified, nervous and scared. The primary feeling was fear – especially of failing family and

friends. Some of Drew's symptoms included a loss of attention, lack of sleep, lack of concentration and fatigue. These
are all classic examples of someone who is suffering from fear
and anxiety.

For Drew a full recovery would occur within a few months of
the counseling. A supportive environment for him to release his
feelings of fear would be crucial to his recovery. Drew's Jewish
background would also play a pivotal role. His faith was important to him, and it was something that helped formed his identity, and therefore would help him when it came to learning how
to cope with his fear and anxiety in healthier ways. The focus
of treatment would be releasing Drew's traumatic experience. I
emphasize traumatic because each situation is different for each
individual. For example, there were young men in Drew's boot
camp class who were able to successfully graduate without any
major psychological stress. Some people perceive situations as
more stressful than others. So we have to honor each person's
fear and how it impacts them.

Part of Drew's success in counseling was that he was able
to fully express all the harmful events that happened to him.
Moreover, because of his time in the counseling office, he
learned that it was okay to express what was on his mind. In
fact, it was very important to his recovery. Even the most hor-
rendous thoughts or feelings are allowed to be expressed,
whether they are accurate or not. We sort those out.

Having grown up attending weekly services and Jewish hol-
idays at the synagogue, Drew was well versed in the Hebrew

Bible (what Christians would call the Old Testament). He began to reflect on how honest and open, not to mention eloquently expressive, the ancient Biblical writers were about their own thoughts and feelings. Especially when it came to either personal or national calamities. For example, Jeremiah, sometimes called "the weeping prophet" because of his many ordeals, authored the biblical book of Lamentations. Drew was quite familiar with these scriptures. In this particular book, the prophet describes the grief of himself and of all of the people over the destruction of Jerusalem by the Babylonians. Nothing is held back or sugar-coated. The grief is real, as genuine as can be, and the prophet expressed it in poetic yet startlingly gritty words.

Drew found this biblical approach to be very compatible with ECT's requirement of dealing head on with grief and other emotional challenges. Whether in ancient times or in the twenty-first century where Drew lives, he now appreciated with a new sense of understanding the many ways that the Jewish faith relies on trust and confidence in God to help bring His people through even the worst of sufferings.

Furthermore, this realization also enabled Drew to put things into perspective, because, as difficult as his current problems may be, they pale in comparison with the history of devastating events in the life of the Jewish people, especially the Holocaust perpetrated by the Nazis. But by tenaciously holding on to their faith, the Jewish people have survived it all and continue to thrive both as individuals and as a people.

This helped to fill Drew with tremendous hope and courage as he moved forward with Emotional Core Therapy.

I gave Drew several examples to practice releasing feelings at home. He was able to choose from a variety of ways to release his feelings. That's what we do with all of our clients. We give them the option to choose what they want to do based on their own world experience and what they like to do.

Some of the ideas include writing, journaling, drawing, listening to music, exercising, jogging, meditation, yoga, or Pilates to name a few. Drew began to feel comfortable in therapy because he chose to freely verbalize his feelings. He started to do more talking, too, which he wasn't used to doing at home, where his family didn't really support expressing his feelings. Once he got into therapy, Drew became more expressive and he started to like it.

Every client is different in how they choose to express themselves. The best way for a therapist to do ECT is to work from a client's perspective and worldview. For Drew, learning to verbalize his unwanted feelings was a huge emotional growth step. He realized over time that it was okay to talk about negative feelings and to show his vulnerabilities. Drew also began to realize the value of cathartically releasing his feelings. He learned how to self-monitor his body for changes in his physical state, and realized that he was getting better as he started to release his feelings. Consequently, his fear level went down.

To examine how ECT helped Drew recover in this situation let's go back to the diagram in Chapter One on authentic feelings. Our brain receives authentic feelings such as fear. Once our brain, which is part of our central nervous system, senses these feelings, the muscles in our body respond. This sequence of events is helpful for our survival as human beings. If you are having trouble understanding this concept think of a situation which has occurred to most of us at home, touching at hot stove. If you accidentally touch a hot stove and burn your finger, you are not likely to repeat this mistake again. Why? We sense the fear as a result of the negative consequence that the action has on our body, i.e., a burnt finger and the accompanying pain. As for Drew, in therapy he learned to monitor his body and to pay attention to his body's feelings. I tried to have Drew monitor his feelings away from the counseling office. By doing this, he was then able to see his debilitating feelings of fear slowly dissipate out of his body.

Another step in Drew's recovery was the use of meditation and relaxation in his life on a daily basis. Drew had nightmares for months prior to entering therapy so it was important for him to learn to have a quiet state of being as part of his daily life. Every person in therapy relaxes in a different way. One person may like sitting in a Jacuzzi, while someone else might like yoga or Pilates, and others might like to do relaxing activities like bowling or walking a dog. The key to relaxing is to have the mind be free of tension, to be able to daydream, to reflect and be able to stay calm. Rather than actually thinking and using your mind actively, we want the mind to freely flow and to reflect. This differs for each person because each person relaxes in a different way.

Another term for relaxation is self-soothing. Everybody self-soothes in different ways so we have to go to their point of view. When we talk about different techniques of relaxation, what's good for one person is not necessarily good for another. You might have a friend, for example, who finds it relaxing to hang out at the mall and can release her feelings that way. But if you're the type who hates crowds, this would not work for you, since you would find it stressful and it would actually make things worse.

So you have to really pay attention to what each person feels helps his or her mind to relax. We have to go back to their history of what they did when they were younger to relax, and we always give people the option of what they want to do to relax. When we examined Drew's history we found that he enjoyed sitting in his room listening to music. While listening to different artists express themselves and their feelings Drew slowly felt his tensions easing away. This process, however, takes time. Once Drew was able to see how authentic feelings operate, he began to release his feelings. His recovery started when he realized that he didn't have to enter boot camp anymore. That was a situation and a relationship that he had entered into but it was separate from himself and he realized that he would never have to go back to it again. That was an important step for him and a critical component of Emotional Core Therapy, realizing that all relationships either grow or weaken. He realized that his relationship with boot camp was in the past, that he was separate from that and he could now start to release that fear. By doing this, Drew was finally able to take back control over his life. Once he understood that he was over this experience he could start to release the pain of it.

All the experiences that Drew had gone through in boot camp were separate from himself. He entered into these relationships and he left them. In therapy, he was reminded that he had succeeded in other events. So why not this event?

Another key for Drew was releasing pain through nature. Things such as trees and water, open land and spaces help the mind to daydream and wander. Imagine yourself sitting under a shady tree on a warm summer day. You listen to the wind blowing and the birds chirping. Looking around you see the beautiful trees of various shapes and sizes, and up above in the sky the beautiful clouds slowly drift past like a soft batch of cotton candy. When you go to this peaceful place you are able to reflect and daydream, allowing your feelings and thoughts to freely wander in and out of your mind.

One question we need to ask is why would Drew not be able to release his feelings? With ECT we recognize that the body has a way of protecting itself from foreign or outside feelings. It is not normal and healthy to have debilitating feelings of fear and loss in our lives. If you don't believe what I'm saying, envision a two year-old girl or boy in a crib. If a two-year-old child has suffered the psychological pain of being yelled at or scolded constantly what would happen? By the same token what would happen if this two-year-old was in his yard and a strange dog came up barking in his face? Quite naturally, the child would start crying to show fear. The child would show visible pain and look for comfort. What would be the remedy? Quite possibly it would be a loving hug from a mommy or daddy or to take the boy away from the dog or the yard where the fearful event had occurred. If bitten, maybe a Band-Aid to stop the bleeding or a visit to the doctor for a shot to make sure that there are no diseases of infections. Every normal and healthy parent would do all that they could to help the child in pain. Why? Because a child cannot do these things themselves, and a two-year-old child cannot lie and deceive themselves about how they feel. They cannot hide pain. They have to release it somehow.

It is a natural process to release emotional pain by crying and whining. They have no defense mechanisms to block the cognitive emotions. Every loving parent would do whatever they could to protect this two-year-old and quite naturally console their pain. Why? The parent loves the child. It is a very powerful relationship.

It is also very important for each one of us to learn how to truly love ourselves. In ECT terms, the definition of loving yourself is to allow yourself a peaceful, meditative, and reflective state of mind throughout the day. The four authentic feelings – joy, grief, fear, and relief – are just temporary states that are certain to change. That is why it is important to not let any of them dominate your emotional self/psyche for too long, if you can help it.

The decision is yours! If you commit to loving yourself (allowing for a peaceful, meditative state of mind) then it becomes much easier to identify and process the four authentic feelings day in and day out. Over time, you learn to release and externalize the feelings of joy, grief, fear, and relief on a daily basis. Learning to love yourself is an important part of growing up, and will serve you well throughout your entire life.

This same power of love is what has to transpire for Drew to get better. He has to respect himself enough to cheer himself and allow himself to get better. It was not a short process for full recovery but so long as Drew had the support of people around him a full recovery was expected. You see, the human body has a natural way of protecting us from danger. The psychological turmoil of sustaining things like fear and loss is dangerous to the human body. Drew has to allow himself to be held, comforted, and supported to be protected, just like this two-year-old. He has to respect himself and his feelings enough to allow himself to heal from this pain.

We are now ready to examine some other scenarios where ECT can help people in your age group to overcome debilitating fear and anxiety. Let's say there is a sixteen-year old boy named Aiden. He had a very happy and ordinary life, up until a few years ago when his parents divorced. He lived with his mother and saw his dad sometimes, though not as often as he would have liked. Then his mom married a guy named Floyd, who seemed decent enough. But the problem was Floyd's son, Jackson, who was about the same age as Aiden. Whereas Aiden was a good kid who worked hard in school, Jackson was the exact opposite. He was basically a slacker, the kind of kid who would get in trouble spending way too much time partying and being an all-around pain in the neck. Worst of all, he would pick on Aiden all the time, calling him names and just plain bullying him every chance he got. It reached the point where Aiden felt like he was falling apart. He couldn't sleep, he couldn't concentrate, had trouble eating and he couldn't feel comfortable around people anymore. If he had to rate his level of fear on a scale of one to ten he would have to say it was a nine or ten, in other words, intolerable.

If Aiden were to go to see a therapist, at first a recommendation would be made to see a medical doctor to decide whether or not medical treatment was needed. With any counseling whether it's ECT or some other form of therapy, professionals always want to make sure their patient's doctor is notified if they desire it. Some will say they do not want to do so, while others will say that's fine. The point is, competent therapists cover all of their bases first.

Since Aiden was a very intelligent boy, the chances would be good that he would be able to identify his authentic feelings pretty quickly in his first couple of months of therapy, along with the real cause of his stress. In ECT therapy, a brief examination of his life would point out to him that he was in control of most of his life. He was happy with his schoolwork, with his after-school job, and with his support group of friends. Aiden also attended a non-denominational Christian church where he had joined a youth group a few years earlier soon after his parents had divorced. The relationship that was causing such debilitating fear, of course, was that with his stepbrother Jackson. Naturally, Aiden already knew that, but in therapy, he would learn how to appropriately release that fear. This might include identifying and making a list of all of the things that were causing him fear and slowly working on reducing fear on each one.

Aiden and his therapist would also work on different techniques for reducing stress. For example, Aiden's penchant for fly-fishing would be excellent for this purpose. When Aiden was fishing, he felt that he was more in control of his life. Slowly over time, this would ease his level of tension and serve as a means of stress relaxation.

As a Christian, Aiden would also be able to turn to prayer as a form of meditation to help relax his mind. His therapist would encourage this, though not any specific prayer or formula. Instead, Aiden will be able to find peace and soothe his soul just by quietly reflecting on what he has learned over the years through Christianity about the goodness of God. ECT helps you have a spiritual relationship with God throughout the day...and who doesn't want that in any religion?

The Bible says that Jesus calls on us to turn over all of our burdens to Him. Aiden finds tremendous solace in that idea, knowing that whatever may happen with his interactions with other people here on earth, His Father in heaven will always be there for him. He is a strong shoulder to cry on as well as the most compassionate Listener in the universe. Aiden can talk with Him anytime day or night – not just when he is in church – and tell his loving Father all of his fears and worries.

Yes, Aiden realizes that God of course already knows all of these things; in fact, He knows everything before the thoughts even form in our minds! But talking to God about his concerns, either in his mind or even out loud when he is all alone, can go a long way towards providing Aiden with the serenity and healing that he is seeking through ECT. His therapist would tell him that he (or she) fully supports that idea, since the ability to let one's mind wander and to meditate is so important to the successful usage of Emotional Core Therapy.

This wouldn't be ideal for everyone but it would work well in this boy's particular case. Why? Because when Aiden is out at the river fishing, he is able to let his mind wander. He daydreams and releases some of his fear-inducing feelings and sorts them out.

Of course, for Aiden as for anybody, there could never be any guarantees. Things do not always work out as planned. Imagine what it must be like for a young couple in their twenties who have a child. Maybe this will be you in just a few years. Instead of being born healthy, however, their child is born with a birth defect or heart defect. The first few years of the couple's relationship is spent at doctor's offices, not sleeping and excessive financial pain. Certainly none of this would have been in all of their happy plans of having a baby! The point is things change as you go forward. In Aiden's case he sought relief from excessive fear. By utilizing some of the ECT techniques used by all therapists to relieve stress, Aiden would stand a good chance of successfully distancing himself from his fear in the same way that Drew had in boot camp.

The difference between Aiden's case and Drew's was that Drew never had to go back to his relationship with stress. Boot camp was over and done. So Drew was able to leave therapy pretty whole. With our fictitious case of Aiden, his stepbrother Jackson would in all likelihood still be belligerent and would not want to himself go to therapy. Bullies like Jackson usually don't think they have a problem – though they clearly do. So as we examine Aiden's situation it is clear that his stepbrother had displayed power over Aiden whenever he could. Aiden felt helpless. In therapy, we would help Aiden to recognize that he needs to work on his own situation separate from his stepbrother. Spending as little time as possible with Jackson would be a big part of the solution.

Time would solve this problem eventually, because the day would come when Aiden would go off to college. Even then, however, Aiden should continue with therapy, as learning ECT would show him new and more varied ways to become calmer. For example, writing, listening to music, and joining the chess club at school would all contribute to a lower level of tension and anxiety. Eventually, through the use of all of these techniques he should hopefully be able to lower his stress to a one or two.

With Emotional Core Therapy, the goal is to help them to see that he/ she has the power to enter and leave relationships. Aiden had spent years not fully understanding his emotions but he never needed professional help before. Now that he has learned how to monitor his body and his authentic feelings he will be able to go on with his life because as he enters young adulthood he will already know how to identify his feelings, recognize toxic relationships and make smart choices to reduce stress. Therapists cannot make decisions for clients, the client has to make decisions about which relationships that they want to enter into. Sometimes people (like the fictional Aiden) have been in a toxic situation. The therapist's job is to be supportive within those situations and try to reduce the stress. The relief may not be instant, but it is in just about every case a step in the right direction.

Emotional Core Therapy is about being human and desiring to stay human. That means honoring and processing the four authentic feelings in all of life's situations. Let's say that there is a fifteen-year old girl named Charlene. She is the star of her school's soccer team. She loves the sport, so that should make her happy, right? Not necessarily. In this case it is actually making her miserable. Why? The pressure of always being the best, of always having to be the one who leads her team to victory, started getting to be too much for Charlene. The pressure was so stressful that she had trouble sleeping, trouble concentrating, had chest pains, mild tension – all of the classic signs of fear or stress. Her heart was beating fast. She had a fear of being a failure. In ECT therapy, it would quickly become apparent that her role on the soccer team was very demanding. Whether it was at practice or in an actual game, Charlene always felt that she was under a microscope. Her coach told Charlene that she was a "natural-born leader" and therefore gave her all kinds of responsibilities on the field. If one of the girls on the team wasn't playing well enough, Charlene was expected to find out why, take the girl under her wing, and improve her soccer skills. A tall order to say the least! At first Charlene liked all of the confidence that had been placed in her by her coach and her teammates, and even the parents and other spectators who attended the games. But after a while it became just too much pressure, and Charlene reached the point where she felt as though she could not take it anymore.

If Charlene were to enter into ECT therapy, one of the benefits would be that she and her therapist would compartmentalize Charlene's stress. She and her therapist would discuss the circumstances and more than likely a common theme would emerge: Charlene's persistent fear of not living up to everyone's expectations. The therapist would review Charlene's history, which would show that she was much more calm back when she was a younger kid. How did things change? One technique that is used in Emotional Core Therapy is to outline the patient's thoughts on a piece of paper, writing down five or maybe even ten different ways that Charlene felt overwhelmed each day. In therapy, Charlene would learn how to process her feelings and then she would be allowed to vent them. This almost always provides at least some momentary relief.

The therapist would also encourage Charlene to incorporate her religious beliefs and practices into her treatment. Charlene's parents were born in India and although Charlene was born in the United States they brought her up with all of the values and teachings of a traditional Hindu family. Like many immigrants, her parents wanted an American name for their daughter, however, they also gave her a Hindu middle name, which was their way of embracing their new home in the U.S. while still retaining a vital connection to their religious and cultural heritage. It was a blending of old and new that in some ways is reflective of how ECT blends the best of both ancient religion and modern psychology to help the people of today.

As she was learning ECT, Charlene recalled some words of wisdom her father had once shared with her from a famous Hindu spiritual teacher named Swami Sivananda. The sagacious teacher taught that we should develop an abiding and childlike trust in God to overcome anxiety. Given her current dilemma, those words really rang home for Charlene! The swami further explained that people are tormented by imaginary reverses and dangers. This affects their present cheerfulness and happiness. To overcome such anxiety, he explained, we should have full faith in God's will.

Charlene also came to further appreciate the way in which Hinduism is more than just a religion, it is a way of life. It is a philosophy that emphasizes that suffering is merely a part of life that leads to self-purification. This helped her to take some of the self-imposed pressure off of herself. Failure is OK. It is all part of the Divine presence. Everything that we do will ultimately, according to the law of karma, contribute to our own personal spiritual growth and betterment.

With these kinds of thoughts in mind, Charlene made herself ready for ECT. She could finally let down her defences and stop worrying about perfection. Instead, as her Hindu beliefs reinforced, her focus needed to shift to Truthfulness (a very important concept in Hinduism), and she soon discovered that ECT is also all about confronting the truth.

Indeed, as Charlene learned more about ECT, she saw that it can only work effectively when a person approaches it with complete honesty. Writing down several different ways she was feeling overwhelmed served as a prime example of this. It would compel Charlene to look deep inside herself and, with the help of her therapist, identify the true sources of her anxiety. Only then, using each step of the ECT process, could she begin to process her emotions and release them in healthy ways. Charlene was pleasantly surprised by how well this method fit in with the traditional Hindu philosophy and way of life she and her family had always practiced.

Of course, so long as Charlene remained on the soccer team, and the coach continued to see her as a "star," there would not be full relief. Charlene's stress level would remain fairly high. Her situation was similar to Aiden's from our second example. Aiden still lived with Jackson, his annoying stepbrother, which was causing him fear. Both of these situations are relationships that these people entered into and they stayed with them, which is why their level of fear remained high. In a perfect world Jackson would have been shipped off to a juvenile detention center and Charlene would have quit the team and both would be happy. But in the real world she wouldn't do that because she cared too much about her coach and her teammates and she didn't want to let them down. Both Aiden and Charlene were stuck in their current circumstances and they were not going to be able to leave anytime soon. Nonetheless, in the short-term they would be able to work on some ECT techniques to effectively release their feelings.

Emotional Core Therapy does not promise utopia or a perfect outcome for every client. Let's keep it real, no therapy can offer that. Oftentimes the best you can do is to deal with your life's stresses head on in a more meaningful and manageable way. For Charlene, if she pursued ECT for a couple of months there is a good possibility that it would allow her to "reframe" her mental state. Instead of saying to herself, *I'm afraid, I'm scared, I'm not doing enough, I'm going to screw up and make my team lose,* Emotional Core Therapy would help Charlene to develop a different mindset. Her frame of thinking would be more like this: *I'm only one part of the team, and I'm doing my part well. My heart is in the right place, it's the pressure to succeed that's causing me excessive fear. I need to recognize that there is more to life than just soccer.* In other words, Charlene needs to create some separation between herself and this sport.

Through ECT we can learn common techniques to reduce stress. For example, Charlene's therapist might suggest for her to practice meditation before games as a way to reclaim herself. One very effective way of practicing meditation is to pay attention to your "calm self." For example, Charlene could review what she did before she became the school's big soccer star that helped her to be peaceful. Working on a calm, steady way to breathe might be one technique. Taking deep short breaths, helps to slow a person's thought processes down. Just plopping down in front of the TV and watching a silly sitcom or mindless "reality show" prior to a soccer game might help Charlene to relax as well. These techniques would help her to slow her body down and clear her mind. ECT would teach Charlene how to monitor her body and start to become calmer.

Keep in mind what Emotional Core Therapy can and cannot do. First and foremost, it helps people to regain their "humanness." But it can never cure cancer, solve all of your problems, or give you all the answers. No therapy can promise these results. Every new relationship we enter into with people, places and things will cause a response from us as human beings. It will either bring joy or fear. That's simply the way life works. With ECT, however, it can be a happier and more peaceful life, and one that we can live with greater dignity and independence. No one can really predict the future. All we can do is work on pursuing joyful relationships and releasing feelings and obtaining a meditative state of calmness most of the time.

Another very common source of stress is the workplace. This can certainly be true for teens as well as for adults. Workplace stress (or school stress) can vary from person to person depending on many factors. Think of jobs that adults have such as a postman or deliveryman. If the person in this job has an injury or condition with his feet and the job requires walking all day, this job would cause excessive stress. What if another individual has no health problems and enjoys nature, being outside, and helping people. In stark contrast, he may love the job. Two different people, same job, yet different levels of stress. That's because people experience stress differently. Still, if you examine the most stressful jobs in our society, most of them cause excessive fear on a normal human's emotions. Look no further than a soldier, policeman, ironworker, professional football player, or a stay at home mother of five, and you will see a common variable. Most of these jobs require a great deal of tasks to be completed, usually in uncomfortable conditions. Thus, they lead to very high levels of stress.

To more closely examine teen workplace stress, let's look at another hypothetical case that we can learn from. This one involves a Junior in high school named Tyler. He stayed busy all day long, both at school and then after school and on weekends working at his father's hardware store. Tyler grew up in a close knit Catholic family – where faith and hard work were always highly valued – and he felt a profound sense of obligation to the family business. But the pressure of putting in so many hours under the watchful (and often critical) eye of his father was getting to Tyler. He was worried about making a mistake that might hurt the business, and he dreaded the idea of disappointing his father. He was also fearful about not having enough money for college if he cut back on his hours on the store. This young man had devoted his life to his family and now it was falling apart.

Tyler exhibited several of the classic symptoms of anxiety: he had trouble sleeping, muscle tension, and he lost weight. With Emotional Core Therapy, Tyler would be encouraged to compartmentalize all of his excessive fears. We would write down each fear and discuss the situation in detail. Part of Tyler' excessive fear was financial stress. He wanted to go to a leading university, but the costs of tuition were staggering. Was the future that he had always dreamed of realistically within his reach? These were not entirely rational thoughts, they were just excessive fears in case the situation went bad.

Over the course of several months of using ECT, Tyler would need to make some key decisions to help bring down his high level of fear. For example, one idea might be to sit down for a serious talk with his father about cutting back on his working hours, explaining to his dad how he could be a more valuable worker if he could just have a little bit more free time to rest and relax. That way he would be less tired and therefore not as worried about messing something up. He might also look into financial aid and scholarships and discover that paying for college will not be as unreachable as he had feared. In other words, ECT would help give Tyler perspective on the whole process of balancing his current work obligations and future college ambitions. He would still be able to work but he would also have to grieve the loss of a certain amount of income. The good news is, identifying this grief would provide Tyler relief from a fearful point of view in that he could rest assured that there would still be a way for him to attend the college of his choice. This relief will lower Tyler's position on the fear scale, maybe dropping it from an eight or nine down to a five or six in a couple of months, and hopefully even lower a few months later.

All therapists want what is best for their clients. But just remember that they can't promise to predict what the future holds in store for you. Tyler would still have to work through his fear and loss, and there is no telling how long that might take. The fact that Tyler was a practicing Catholic would also help him to process his emotions in healthy ways and to conquer his fears. In the Catholic tradition, God intervenes in the lives of human beings in a number of ways, including when He provides the protection of His saints and angels. For Tyler, he had always felt a close connection to Michael the Archangel, whom the Church says is a protector of the faithful. One sentence of a longer prayer to Michael the Archangel that Tyler would keep at the forefront of his mind and close to his heart throughout the day reads: "Be our safeguard against the wickedness and snares of the devil."

Tyler also wore a chain around his neck with a pendant in the form of the traditional depiction of Michael the Archangel wielding a sword. It is not meant as a violent image; to the contrary, it is symbolic of the fact that God loves us so much that He sends His holy angels down to earth to protect us from harm and guide us home to heaven. That was a very comforting thought for Tyler, and he would often gently hold the pendant and look at it with eyes of faith as he poured his heart out to God in silent prayer and meditation.

Now, this approach may not work for every person using ECT, or for all religious people because, of course, every situation is different. As we have seen with other situations in this book, sometimes the road to recovery can be long and hard. Fortunately, Emotional Core Therapy offers a path, a strategy for coping that helps us not only with major crises, but also with the less drastic (but every bit as real) worries and stressors that all of us contend with in our everyday lives.

Hopefully the "FEAR" you have about comprehending this approach has been alleviated somewhat after reading the anxiety chapter. Feel free to glance at the adjacent flowchart to measure your comprehension of the psychological process we are teaching in this book. Don't worry (otherwise known as fear) if you haven't mastered the entire approach just yet. We will revisit the approach in more detail in the following chapter, "Using ECT to Understand Anger."

List Five Relationships That You Have Entered That Have Caused You Fear

A) TAKING THE SAT EXAM

B) GOING ON A ROLLER COASTER.

1.

2.

3.

4.

5.

Notes:

List Five Ways You Can Release Debilitating Feelings Of Fear.

A) READ COMIC BOOKS OR SOMETHING FUNNY

B) CALL AN OLD FRIEND WHO HAS MOVED AWAY AND CATCH UP ON STUFF

1.

2.

3.

4.

5.

Notes:

SYMPTOMS OF ANXIETY

HAVING AN INCREASED HEART RATE

BREATHING RAPIDLY (HYPERVENTILATION)

FEELING POWERLESS

HAVING A SENSE OF IMPENDING DANGER, PANIC OR DOOM

FEELING APPREHENSIVE

SWEATING

FEELING WEAK OR FATIGUED

TREMBLING

List Five Of Your Own Symptoms Of Anxiety

1.

2.

3.

4.

5.

Notes:

ECT Flow Chart

Relationships;
self, other people, places, things

⬇

Needs;
emotional, financial, spiritual, physical

⬇

Five Senses;
seeing, touching, smelling, tasting, hearing

⬇

Four Authentic Feelings;
joy, grief, fear, relief

⬇

Effects;
brain/central nervous system

⬇

Uncomfortable Symptoms;
muscle tightness, fatigue, etc.

⬇

Releasing Process;
learn to discharge toxic feelings

⬇

Balancing Your Equilibrium;
practice various daily meditative techniques

CHAPTER FOUR
Using ECT To Understand Anger

So far, we've mostly been exploring situations where someone has hurt our feelings or harmed us in some way. But as I am sure that you will admit, on occasion you too have had episodes when you lose your temper and get angry with other people, sometimes in a way that may be hurtful. We all have done so from at one point or another. That doesn't make you a bad person. It just means that we all have faults in relationships. There are instances when we accidentally or intentionally hurt others in our lives. Examples might be inappropriately talking back to your parents, using force to intimidate other kids at school, or telling mean jokes at somebody else's expense.

All of us do something like this at least once in a while. The difference, however, between an emotionally healthy person and an abusive person is that the emotionally healthy person truly regrets doing the hurtful or harmful act. Why?

They know that hurting someone is destructive in nature. Have you ever heard the saying, "Treat others as you want to be treated"? It really makes a lot of sense if you think about it, and this same sense of fairness and respect for others can be seen using the techniques of Emotional Core Therapy. With ECT we understand that it is entering and leaving relationships that cause stress (otherwise known as debilitating feelings of fear and grief). As we discussed earlier in the book, when we go towards a relationship we like (such as a good friend) there is joy. When we leave something we like (for example, that same good friend) there is grief. When we go towards something we dislike (for instance, taking an exam that we did not prepare for) there is fear. When we leave something we dislike (finishing the exam and receiving a decent grade on it) there is relief. Since anger is a reaction to grief, what relationship is being stressed? The answer is the relationship that you have with yourself. In the hypothetical cases you will read in this chapter keep in mind that each character who is angry is really grieving his own sense of loss. That is the important point that I want you to keep in time.

We all from time to time have made mistakes that hurt others and brought grief or fear into others' lives. Examples might include arguing with your parents, or "blowing up" at your friends at school. The difference is that when you begin to honor your authentic feelings of joy, grief, fear, and relief, you become aware of your uncomfortable muscle and bodily sensations that result from stress. This physical discomfort is a signal that something is wrong with a relationship. With

ECT, we recognize that our normal state of being is one of meditation or relaxation. Hence, we become trained to eliminate the debilitating feelings of fear and loss.

Anger is a reaction to grief. People who are angry are in fact, grieving and suffering loss. Each individual varies in their intensity and duration of anger. One of the benefits of using ECT is it helps give us a better grasp of authentic feelings, so we can dig deeper and get to the real roots of someone's anger. We must also realize that anger can affect the central nervous system, so it's important especially as we get older to have less stress on the body, and less anger in one's life. By having less anger and stress, your blood pressure can stay calm and your body can be more regulated.

Let's take the fictional example of an angry sixteen-year old boy to see how ECT can help him better his communication skills and in turn get his needs met. The young man in this hypothetical case, Connor, often loses his temper with his twelve-year old brother, Ethan. "You moron! I already showed you how to do that math problem three times, stop asking me to help you again you dummy." Wow! Can't you just feel the harmful and destructive power of those words as you read them?

With Emotional Core Therapy, Connor would be taught to honor himself as well as others. A better way of stating his grief of constantly be asked the same homework questions over and over by his little brother might be by saying something like this: "Ethan, I am really unhappy when I have to keep repeating stuff. I'm disappointed because I know how smart you are. But you're just using my answers to finish your homework instead of really learning the math the way that you are supposed to learn it." It doesn't have to be these exact words, but something that conveys this sentiment in a similar non-accusatory yet frankly honest manner. These kinds of words would be much more likely to draw Connor's little brother into a conversation that might actually solve the problem. In stark contrast, by Connor getting angry and sarcastic, the two of them will just end up fighting and mis-understanding each other even more. The more authentic these two brothers can be with each other, the closer they will become in their relationship. As people become better at authenticating their four feelings of joy, grief, fear, and relief, they can learn to grow their relationships further and better.

Religious beliefs can be very helpful for anybody, includ-ing teenagers, when it comes to dealing with their emotions, particularly when it involves family members. Connor and his family belonged to the Church of Jesus Christ of Latter Day Saints (the LDS Church), also known as the Mormons. He had always been taught that the teachings of the Book of Mormon, along with the Bible, would give him practical advice for dealing with the everyday issues of life. So, along with prac-ticing ECT, Connor searched the scriptures. In the Book of Mormon's "Book of Nephi," he came across the following pas-sage, which truly resonated with him: "Behold, this is not my doctrine, to stir up the hearts of men with anger, one against another; but *this* is my doctrine, that such things should be done away." Reading that passage helped to encourage Connor that learning to deal with his anger issues in healthier ways would be pleasing to God, which strongly motivated him to pursue ECT as vigorously as possible.

ECT would probably not only help Connor to get along better with Ethan, it would help him to evolve as a human being too. It would allow him to use more authentic words such as "unhappy" and "disappointed" instead of "moron" and "dummy." These words should help Connor to get in touch with his inner self. The sooner he gets in touch with his core feelings, the sooner he can release them and move on to a healthier state of being. The beauty of ECT is the ability to make the hundreds of feelings simplified into one of the four authentic feelings. By doing so, one has a much better chance of releasing psychic pain and moving on from the negative state of being.

Again, when it came to this issue of his inner self, Connor turned to his faith to buttress what he was learning through ECT. Indeed, prayerful reflection and reading religious literature could change Connor's perspective on how he sees himself and others. As part of this pursuit, he read something written in *Ensign* magazine, published by the LDS Church, that fit in perfectly with the new way of thinking he was developing: "Harmony in the home can increase when we ask the Lord in both our family and personal prayers to help us see each other differently and control our negative feelings."

Connor felt as though those words were speaking to him directly, and he began to think differently about both himself and his little brother. He realized that he could be a strong role model for Ethan, and he prayed to God to help him to change the way he spoke and the choice of words he used with his little brother. Connor knew this would have a positive influence not only on his younger sibling's life, but on his own life, too. He really did not want to go around every day living with anger and being mean, and with prayer and ECT he soon realized that there was indeed a different way to live.

As Connor becomes more emotionally centered, there is less chance that he will turn to the use of anger, as anger is nothing more than a reaction to one of the four authentic feelings. When you learn to live in a more authentic way, honoring your feelings, you become less inclined to need anger as a response to relationships. Why would one use anger as a means of communication when there are far better, less destructive options available?

Our next example of anger is the hypothetical case of a fourteen-year old girl named Huan, who is the youngest of four children. Her mother is a single mom who works hard, but the family always seems to be struggling to make ends meet financially. That means Huan gets a lot of hand-me-down clothes from her older sisters rather than the cool new designer fashions that many of her friends are always wearing. One day when Huan asks her mom for money to buy this awesome new pair of jeans she saw at the mall, her mother gently explains that they are too expensive. Turned down again! Huan explodes in a fit of anger. "That's so unfair, Mom! All my friends dress like supermodels and I have to wear dorky Old School clothes that make me look like such a dweeb! Why are we always so broke?"

Of course, later on Huan feels terrible about how insensitive she was when she blew up at her mom. She loves her mother very much and feels awful that she can't control her anger. Respecting elders and of course her parents has always been an important part of Huan's upbringing in a family that emphasized traditional Chinese values and the Buddhist religion. Using ECT, we would examine the situation for the four authentic feelings. Anger is not one of the four authentic feelings, so what was Huan really feeling? Huan had obviously been very hurt when she heard the bad news that once again she would have to settle for second best when it came to clothing. Her feeling of grief came from her perception that maybe this time, somehow things would be different. In her mind she had envisioned asking her mother for the money for the new jeans, and her mother saying that yes, she was going to let her daughter buy whatever she wanted this time. But what she was really grieving was the loss of feeling respected by all of her classmates. Huan felt like everyone thought that her family was some kind of "poverty case," and she was sad and embarrassed about it. Simply put, Huan was deeply hurt, but she did not know how to process her feelings appropriately.

Let's examine how Huan could approach this situation if she had learned about Emotional Core Therapy and using the four authentic feelings. She might say, "Hi, Mom, I want to talk to you about something. I know that you've been kinda down and having a tough time with money, and it's been making me sad and upset too. But I have an idea for buying some new clothes I saw at the mall. I can save up half of the money from babysitting and maybe you can give me the other half?"

This alternative approach would be much better than saying, "That's so unfair, Mom! Why are we always so broke?" With this new statement, Huan is acknowledging her mother's circumstances and also her own authentic feelings. "Sad" and "upset" are really just different ways to describe grief. That is why in the second example where Huan shares her feelings with her mother, Huan had a better chance of drawing her mom into the conversation and they just might end up actually understanding each other for a change.

As part of this process, Huan was also practicing the Buddhist concept of "mindfulness," which fits in very nicely with ECT. She had been taught that mindfulness helps a person to keep in touch with their "stream of consciousness."

This kind of awareness is essential to understanding Buddhism and living by its principles. The Buddhist trait of "sati" involves "moment to moment awareness of present events." Many see it as a path towards spiritual liberation. For Huan, it offered a very practical way to implement on a daily basis what she had been learning through ECT. She was able to quiet her mind through peaceful meditation by using mindfulness.

The key to mindfulness is keeping oneself in the present moment rather than letting fear and depressing thoughts pre-occupy your thinking. It was an excellent fit with the approach and goals of ECT that Huan was learning. In fact, the more she learned about ECT, the more she came to understand that such meditation could be an important addition to her toolbox of techniques that she was compiling for finally dealing properly with her anger issues.

During meditation, Huan would sit in a comfortable chair and begin by concentrating only on her breathing, in and out slowly through her nostrils and feeling the gentle rise and fall of her abdomen. When her thoughts would begin to wander, she would merely return them to the simple act of breathing. This brought about the desired effect of bringing stillness and quietude to her mind. It put her into a mental state that was non-judgmental (a key Buddhist concept) and detached from distracting thoughts of self-criticism or feelings of being hurt by the past actions of others. This helped Huan to process her emotions in a much healthier way, just as she was discovering by learning and using the ECT process.

Mindfulness is a highly effective technique to calm the central nervous system down. Over the years, I have seen clients make better decisions when they have a calmer state of being. That being said, mindfulness is one of many excellent meditative exercises one can do to bring tranquility in their lives. ECT strives to work from a client's perspective so with each new client we research their history. We try to find what has worked in the past and what each client is comfortable in doing as a meditation exercise. As a reminder, a meditative lifestyle and state of being, is the eighth step of the ECT Flowchart. We may not always be able to achieve this goal on a day to day basis, but the more we make an effort to stay calm and relaxed and make mental health a priority in life, the better chance we have of identifying stress.

Huan had no reason to focus on anger or resentment; instead, as ECT encourages, she allowed her mind to concentrate on thoughts and images that made her happy. She even laughed when she recalled that her name, Huan, meant "happy" in Chinese. Yes, her anger might be an inevitable part of being human, but Huan was gradually learning that she did not have to give it the power to control her. In fact, with her Buddhist faith and ECT, she would feel more empowered than ever when it came to dealing with her emotions in healthy ways.

Anger pulls people away from each other and injects fear into the dialogue and it detracts from healthy communication with other human beings. In the long run, Huan will have a much better relationship with her mom if she can encourage meaningful conversations with her rather than losing her temper and making both of them upset.

Another hypothetical example of someone using anger inappropriately involves George, a high school senior who is on the verge of breaking up with Christie, his long-time girlfriend. Bitter, angry and jealous, George has lashed out verbally at Christie, calling her all kinds of terrible names, including in front of other people. He (falsely) accused her of "running around" and branded her a "tramp."

This hate-fuelled behavior was not at all like George's typical demeanor, which was usually carefree and easy-going. People who knew George at the Greek Orthodox parish he had attended since he was a little boy would be shocked if they heard his cruel ranting. What went wrong? What might be the true root of all of that anger? What was the source of his anger? In Emotional Core Therapy, George and his therapist would find out more about his past and how it related to what was currently going on his life. For example, did his sense of self-esteem and self-value come from having a girlfriend? If so, potentially losing Christie would be even more traumatic for him than a breakup would be otherwise. In fact, the sense of loss might be downright unbearable.

The key to recovery would be for George to begin to process his feelings more and more. Rather than dwell on the loss, it would be important for him to acknowledge it and then to properly "mourn" it. In these kinds of cases, further examination of one's authentic feelings often reveals some hard truths that a person may have been reluctant to admit to prior to therapy. For example, it might come out that George's treatment of his girlfriend had been less than kind for a very long time, in fact, long before their breakup became imminent. He would always act possessive and jealous whenever she was around other boys, even though clearly it was completely innocent on her part. In other words, his own insecurities and fears about his own shortcomings were getting the better of George and basically turning him into a mean and controlling bully.

With ECT, George's therapist would help him to recognize that he had a powerful sense of loss when it came to his relationship with Christie. He would then be able to begin to honor his feelings and change his vocabulary. For example, he might start to use statements like, "I feel grief when my feelings are not respected," or, "I feel a sense of loss when it seems like I'm not appreciated." He could also begin to change his behaviors that were causing him grief and loss, and to show Christie more respect too.

George would also be encouraged to turn to his faith as not only a means of comfort, but also as an additional support for what he was learning about anger through ECT. In the Greek Orthodox tradition, anger is seen as an evil that we must combat. In the Bible (Ephesians 4: 26-27), George read: "Do not let the sun go down upon your anger: and do not make room for the devil". In other words, George realized that it was not only beneficial to his mental health, but also to his spiritual health as well to find ways to dispense with his anger and act with more kindness to those around him, especially his loved ones to whom he was the closest. George did not want to open the door and "make room" for evil to enter his life – and he knew that his anger represented that open door. Fortunately, through the combined benefits of ECT and embracing his faith more fully than ever before, George was now discovering ways to get down to the roots of his anger so that he could finally properly deal with it.

Moreover, as part of learning the ECT process, George knew that peaceful thoughts and imagery were essential for quieting his mind and entering the relaxed state that all of us need for our own well-being. To this end, George did not turn to formulaic prayers. Instead, he repeated simple phrases like, "Christ's love transform me," while focusing on (either in his mind or by looking at an actual picture) an icon of Jesus. Icons are very important in the Greek Orthodox Church. Orthodox believers like George consider them "windows to heaven" and they are meant to depict the peace and serenity of Christ. This perfectly mirrored the peace and serenity that George was seeking in his own heart.

As therapists we are trained to look for growth. But it's important to note that the exact amount of growth always varies from one person to the next. Some clients want to learn all that they can to get better. If ECT was learning the alphabet, some clients would want to learn from A to Z, while others would only want to learn A through P. Therapy has to be supportive of each client no matter what state of life they are in.

Let's consider another fictitious case of a young person with anger issues who could benefit from ECT. This time it involves a nineteen-year old boy named Raoul. Fleeing a life of poverty in Guatemala, Raoul arrived in New York City alone on his eighteenth birthday. He quickly got a job at a fast food restaurant, and by being such a hard worker, he soon became the manager, in charge of a mostly teenage kitchen crew. Raoul worked very long hours in the hot kitchen and he became very harsh with the kids who worked for him, yelling at them for even the smallest of mistakes. He was especially tough on a timid new employee named Valerie. Raoul would call her names, devalue her role as a worker and belittle her in front of the other employees.

What might be behind this kind of obnoxious behavior? We would explore that question in Emotional Core Therapy and we might find, for example, that being verbally harsh and demanding gave Raoul a sense of power and control that was lacking in other areas of his life. Maybe he had very few friends or even acquaintances outside of work. In other words, he had no support system. One of the first things the ECT therapist would do would be to start the process of releasing Raoul's feelings. It may be that he had never had an opportunity to tell anyone how he felt deep inside, especially how fearful he felt. Alone in a new country, he had a sense that he was considered "at the bottom of the totem pole." He did not speak English very well and often felt like an outsider. This led to feelings of frustration that he vented onto those around him in angry outbursts.

Through counseling in ECT, Raoul would begin to heal his relationship with Valerie and all of the other people who worked under him. But ECT would do this by helping Raoul to realize certain things about himself. For starters, he would be encouraged to make friends outside of work. This way the kids at the restaurant wouldn't be the only people in his life. Once he had more friends, Raoul would be able to authentically share how he was feeling. He could share his deeper feelings of loss and grief.

Another way for Raoul to share his feelings came through his Catholic faith, which he had been brought up with back home in Guatemala. Though he had fallen away from the Church in recent years and did not attend mass very often, Raoul now began attending services every Sunday at a parish in his neighborhood that conducted masses in his native Spanish language.

He felt a real connection with the elderly priest, himself an immigrant who in his homilies often spoke of his own struggles as a newcomer to America. Raoul also began going to confession on a regular basis (which Catholics now call the Sacrament of Reconciliation). This gave him an opportunity to tell another human being (in this case the priest) all that was troubling his mind, and when given absolution (forgiveness of sins) he was able to deal more effectively with his feelings of loss and grief, rather than simply feeling guilty about them.

Raoul's renewed interest in his Catholic faith also provided him with a powerful sense of community, outside of work, that he did not have before. He joined a youth group where he made some great new friends, and he volunteered at the parish food pantry. Having lived in grinding poverty himself for most of his young life, Raoul was now able to redirect some of his "angry energy" into a positive direction by helping those in need.

Furthermore, as he continued to gain new insights about himself through ECT, Raoul took comfort in Catholicism's portrayal of Jesus as a gentle shepherd who devoted His life to nurturing and protecting His flock. The Bible even described God as "slow to anger." The beautiful imagery that these peaceful concepts spawned in Raoul's mind inspired him to try to live by these same ideals. The more he understood about the person he had become, and who he wanted to be, the more Raoul became dedicated to working closely with his therapist to make better choices and to develop into the kind of young man that he strongly felt his newfound faith was calling him to be.

Over time, Raoul would recognize that he would need to work as hard as he could on being authentic with his feelings, as that would be the key to keeping his anger under control. Emotional Core Therapy would also help him to recognize that being lonely was something that he could change.

The goal of ECT as with any therapy is to make you more independent and empowered. Identifying one's feelings in therapy is a big step forward, but it's even more important to make this become a part of your everyday life. The more you have support and friends the less you will be alone. This would help someone like Raoul to identify and understand that his displays of anger were really expressions of loss and grief. He could then begin to monitor his feelings of anger each day. For example, every time he would start to feel angry he would ask himself, what am I losing? What am I grieving?

In Emotional Core Therapy, Raoul's therapist would look at his previous history to help him find ways to relax and release his feelings. This could involve outdoor activities such as bike riding or maybe he could take up a hobby such as painting, especially if that was something that he had done in the past that he found relaxing. Journaling and writing can also be used to help release the toxic pain of loss, as a person like Raoul probably feels like he left a lot behind in his home country trying to make a new life for himself in America. These kinds of pent up feelings can easily lead to excessive anger. Once Raoul learns to release his feelings in an authentic and healthy manner, and he will start to feel more comfortable with himself. All of these techniques would very likely improve his communication style, which in turn would make him a better boss at work – somebody that the other workers would like and respect rather than fear and loathe.

Over many years of doing therapy, I am constantly reminded of the humanness of all of us. In my private practice setting, I usually don't work with the serious or profoundly emotionally disturbed. Yet I do have clients who come to me with a wide range of mental health conditions. Some clients who seek treatment have been classified or diagnosed in their past as having Attention Deficit Disorder, Bipolar Disorder, Narcissistic Disorder and Obsessive Disorder. Others have sought treatment for self-mutilation issues such as cutting themselves. Some clients have suffered sexual trauma and sexual dysfunction issues. In my experience, ECT can help a broad spectrum of these types of mental health issues that are mild in scope when used with other therapy techniques besides ECT. Why? ECT utilizes core techniques that are common to most humans. For example, who has not suffered feelings of loss or fear? Who cannot benefit from learning various relaxation techniques? When would learning how to release feelings be detrimental to a client?

What I have found is that I utilize many different techniques (other than ECT) for clients that have more moderate to severe personality problems. This is primarily because of resistance to change. Oftentimes you need a variety of psychological techniques to help the more resistant client to grow. In many cases, more energy and focus is needed to bring about positive outcomes with clients who are suffering serious mental health issues. Serious cases of depression, anxiety, and anger would likely benefit from a similar approach for the same reason.

Any psychological technique that can successfully release emotions is helpful in treatment. ECT is very inclusive of other therapy approaches that can release emotions such as EMDR, biofeedback, hypnosis, art therapy, to name a few.

Unfortunately, mentioning these would go beyond the scope of this book. I would like to point out that common everyday relaxation techniques like yoga and Pilates can be used with ECT to relax.

One of my favorite movies about hope and optimism is "The Shawshank Redemption." The main character in the movie never gave up hope about getting out of prison. His love of life was so strong that he never gave up on his dream to live his life in freedom. His will was so strong that he spent years and years chiseling rock inside his jail cell. I would like our readers to feel the same way about life. Life is so precious, why not live every day to its fullest. For this prisoner it was a life or death attitude and he chose to live – therefore he chose a way to escape out of prison.

ECT provides such a path by allowing us to relinquish toxic pain and negative energy. Remember the rudderless rowboat? What kind of rowboat would you prefer to float around in? One with water seeping in the sides and slowing the boat down? Or one that glides effortlessly through the water?

One of the awesome results of learning ECT is that it makes you realize that no one gets a free ride in life if they aspire to stay healthy and human. You can't kill, steal, or harm someone else, without feeling guilty (in other words, having a sense of loss). Why? The feelings of loss will stay inside you and not be released. Remember, the key point of ECT is to live in a meditative and relaxed state of being. In order to do ECT properly one has to monitor and release all four authentic feelings on a daily basis. Being stuck in a state of grief can be a real drag.

Earlier in the book we discussed how you could gauge someone's success in learning Emotional Core Therapy. The more you can learn and acquire the steps of the ECT flow-chart the more confident you will feel about yourself. This book is not about becoming a leader, gaining fame or fortune. Most of the people who assume high levels of responsibility also have high levels of stress (otherwise known as fear). They have excessive fear because they have too many responsibilities and too many tasks.

I want my clients to have power, and to be able to handle their responsibilities without excessive fear or stress. ECT allows clients to get a grasp on what they can and can't handle when it comes to various situations in life, and this is true regardless of your age. Oftentimes, when someone is overly fearful or stressed, anger comes out. The more you become comfortable with the ECT process, the less chance you will become angry. That's because you learn to process your feelings better. Since anger is not an authentic feeling anyway, there becomes less of a need to use anger. Emotionally healthy people can express feelings of sadness, just as readily as feelings of joy. The point is, they are being true to themselves, which is precisely what makes them emotionally healthy in the first place.

List five relationships / events that have caused you anger (which is a reaction to grief)

A) SOMEONE CHEATING WHEN YOU'RE PLAYING A SPORT

B) SOMEONE TELLING YOU TO "SHUT UP"

1.

2.

3.

4.

5.

Notes:

List five ways that allow you to appropriately process your anger (which is a reaction to grief)

A) I FEEL SAD WHEN YOU DEMAND MY TIME AND ENERGY WITHOUT SAYING THANK YOU.

B) I AM HURT (ANOTHER WORD FOR GRIEF) THAT YOU BORROW MY MONEY WITHOUT PAYING ME BACK.

1.

2.

3.

4.

5.

Notes:

SYMPTOMS OF ANGER

FEELING HOT AND FLUSHED

RACING HEARTBEAT

TENSION IN SHOULDERS AND NECK

FEELING AGITATED

List Five Of Your Own Symptoms Of Anger

1.

2.

3.

4.

5.

Notes:

ECT Flow Chart

Relationships;
self, other people, places, things

⬇

Needs;
emotional, financial, spiritual, physical

⬇

Five Senses;
seeing, touching, smelling, tasting, hearing

⬇

Four Authentic Feelings;
joy, grief, fear, relief

⬇

Effects;
brain/central nervous system

⬇

Uncomfortable Symptoms;
muscle tightness, fatigue, etc.

⬇

Releasing Process;
learn to discharge toxic feelings

⬇

Balancing Your Equilibrium;
practice various daily meditative techniques

CHAPTER FIVE
Using ECT to Help Couples

As we begin to discuss how Emotional Core Therapy can help couples, I want to highlight an important reason why everyone would benefit from using ECT. Especially if you were brought up in one of the colder areas of the country, you probably remember how your parents were on your case making sure that you dress warm during the winter. Now that you are older you know what their reason was. Protection. You can get sick and be subjected to long term damage when you are out in the cold for long periods of time without adequate protection. In much the same way, you can think of Emotional Core Therapy as an ideal way of protecting yourself from the inevitable harm that accompanies the arrival of debilitating stress. Whether you like it or not, you will suffer fear and loss in your life. In fact, most of us will have at least some minor irritation on a daily or weekly basis. On a larger scale, you are old enough now to take a serious look at our world and see that it is full of problems that cause people all kinds of traumatic states of fear and grief. I'm not trying to be bleak or pessimistic, just realistic about the challenges facing you as an individual and your generation collectively.

Emotional Core Therapy can help you to meet those challenges head on. It is an easy to use technique (once you understand it) technique for protecting human beings from the "harmful cold weather" known as stress. I believe that education is the key. People realize that emotional trauma is a national epidemic but no one knows how to fix the problem. When I see the hundreds of psychology books for sale that take an advanced degree to comprehend, it becomes clear why a solution has not been found. There needs to be a self-help book that every literate person can read. To that extent, I have tried at great lengths to keep this ECT book reader friendly.

As we begin this chapter on couples we will again see how ECT can bring "joy" to your life, in this case by helping you with love relationships. Nearly all of us know the story of Romeo and Juliet. They had deep and eternal love. It seemed like the two lovebirds never failed to keep the spark or chemistry going in their relationship, no matter what difficulties came between them. The only problem with this love tragedy is that it is not very realistic. That is where Emotional Core Therapy steps in. It shows us how two people can build a realistic partnership better by using better communication patterns.

Before I discuss a few (mostly hypothetical) scenarios where ECT helped young couples navigate through their lives, I want to point out that I see lots of people in therapy that seem very happy with their lives being single. Being "in a relationship" is not some sort of automatic guarantee of perfect, trouble-free happiness. As a matter of fact, there are even benefits to remaining single for a period of time. You get to know to learn and love yourself without having the demands of a partner on a daily basis. Still, others recognize that they have a better chance of getting all of their needs met through a committed relationship. Since ECT deals with authentic feelings, there is no difference in treatment of couples of various ethnicities, heterosexual or homosexual. Emotional, financial, spiritual, and physical needs as we already know vary from person to person. I've discovered the benefits of focusing on authentic feelings in a relationship takes away from biases of both the client and therapists.

In this chapter we begin to see more clearly what brings us stress in our relationships from the perspective of both young men and young women. It is the "needs" and "demands" that each partner brings to the relationship that cause us to have one of the four authentic feelings. In our ECT Flowchart, we see that needs are broken down to four areas. These are emotional, financial, spiritual, and physical. We have organized needs into these four areas because they provide a simple structure for us to understand what causes us stress. There are literally millions of stresses in relationships. Don't worry,

I'm not going to discuss every single one of them! For the sake of simplicity, we break them down into one of four areas.

The first couple I want to discuss is Blake and Jenny. This hypothetical couple were seniors in high school who had been dating fairly seriously for about a year. In the last few months, though, things had been going downhill fast and they found themselves arguing more often than not. Blake never seemed to listen to Jenny's concerns. Her family was not as well off financially as Blake's family, and she was worried about going to a good college next year. Blake on the other hand only wanted to party and have fun in his senior year of high school, rather than worrying about more serious things in the future.

Things started to go from bad to worse when Jenny told Blake that she thought they should end their relationship. Blake was stunned and insisted that they should remain a couple. If they both agreed to see a therapist to find out if they could work out their problems and stay together, ECT might be able to help them. Therapy would reveal that Jenny's statement of emotional pain regarding her future was clearly based on her authentic feelings of grief. She was grieving the ideal of a financially secure college career along with a strong and potentially lasting relationship with Blake. In addition, she had a lot of fear regarding her future: wonder if she had to settle for a second rate college? How much might that damage her career?

The focus of the treatment with both Jenny and Blake would be to highlight the authentic feelings of fear and loss that Jenny faced. By listening to her processing her feelings it started to become apparent that there was more than one-way Jenny felt loss and fear. She was also grieving the potential loss of ever attaining her ideal job, a happy relationship with Blake and most of all, Jenny was grieving the loss of a young man who cared and listened to her.

Though neither Jenny nor Blake had been brought up in deeply religious families, they did both consider themselves Christians and they felt that embracing spirituality might help resolve some of their inner problems. They began attending a non-denominational church where the minister often emphasized placing all of your trust in Jesus. This really struck a chord in the young couple. For Jenny in particular, rather than worry about the future, she started to view it as something that she should look forward to with joy.

Worries would not go away completely for either of them of course, but the more they explored Christian beliefs, they came to understand what Jesus taught His followers about these issues. For example, as part of the famous Sermon on the Mount, He proclaimed: "Therefore I tell you, do not worry about your life, what you will eat or drink; or about your body, what you will wear. Is not life more than food, and the body more than clothes?"

They had a conversation about this scripture reading after church services one day. Blake and Jenny agreed that, even though it was true that they needed to be responsible in thinking about their futures, they also needed to place their faith and trust in God that, one way or the other, things would work out for the best for them, both as individuals and as a couple.

The two young people's new emphasis on faith would also help them to deal more effectively with Blake's issues. Using ECT, it would soon become apparent that Blake had difficulty emotionally connecting with girls. Despite his outwardly cocky personality, deep inside he was insecure about his own shortcomings and worried that he could never live up to Jenny's high standards and expectations. He was running away from the future rather than facing it head on. In church, however, the minister often preached that Jesus accepts people just as they are; all that He requires is their simple belief and trust in Him.

Blake took this concept into his heart, and into his mind. Rather than complex prayers, he engaged in meditation, sitting quietly and in his mind's eye envisioning a cross. Aloud, he continuously repeated something he was hearing in church a lot, the phrase: "Let go and let God." That helped tremendously to calm his mind.

If I were helping a couple like this, I would have them make a list of what each needed at different levels (emotional, financial, spiritual and physical) from each other. We would then discuss on a weekly basis, the efforts to meet each partner's needs, spending equal time in therapy stressing each person's needs, and not being just one sided. In other words, we would spend half the time on Jenny and half on

Blake. Successful relationships are the result of mature couples meeting each other's needs. Of course, couples in high school all have some more maturing to do, and this almost certainly would be a contributing factor in Jenny and Blake's problems. Blake was used to basically living as a kid and just was not ready to start concerning himself with adult problems and issues. Yet this was not what Jenny needed at all. Blake had difficulty really paying attention to the emotional feeling of loss that Jenny was displaying on a daily basis. He also had difficulty relating to her excessive fear. ECT would likely reveal that Blake continually tried to hide himself in partying and lots of fun stuff to escape his authentic feelings of grief.

In order to receive any benefit from therapy, Jenny would need to assert her feelings. It would be important for both of them to spend time working hard on making sure each other's feelings were heard, in the authentic feelings of joy, grief, fear and relief.

Emotional Core Therapy could be successful for both Jenny and Blake if they could both learn to understand and respect each other's authentic feelings. Most critically, Jenny would need to rid herself of toxic feelings of loss and grief. As for Blake, he was truly happy in his relationship except for not being able to please Jenny. He really didn't have a lot of excess needs himself that needed to be met so in therapy they would be able to focus a lot on alleviating Jenny's pain.

Emotional Core Therapy can give hope to a couple in therapy, as it matches authentic feelings with the needs of partners. Most couples can learn a process of being authentic in their feelings by using ECT. When ECT is used with couples, it can bring them closer together and they both can learn at the same time the different techniques of ECT. In other words, they both can help each learn it in addition to the therapist helping them. As a relationship builds, ECT is also helpful in building independence for both partners, which is always especially important for young people. They both can work on finding peace for themselves, a vital component for all healthy relationships. When you have peace in your life and you work on it every day, you start to work on vitality and vigor which is basically a sign of power. We want both partners in therapy to have as much power as they want and to feel as vibrant as possible. That only comes from being emotionally balanced.

Examining each relationship through the eyes of Emotional Core Therapy, we see that healthy relationships honor the four authentic feelings of joy, grief, fear, and relief. A healthy relationship recognizes that the individual may need space to relax and have time for himself/herself. When you can finally begin to understand this key point of ECT, you can begin to have "real and authentic" power. Power you can count on long-term. Relationships that last a long time.

The second couple I would like to highlight is a young couple named Jeff and Kim, recent high school graduates who decided to live together before getting married. The names have been changed but their story is true. Both were very energetic and optimistic young people. They were both successful at work and had a great group of friends. Both were very popular in the office and their respective work-places. They were both quite attracted to each other and obviously very committed to each other. So what could possibly be wrong that such a vibrant and strong young couple would need to see a marital therapist? Why would they blow up and get so mad at each from time to time? How would ECT be able to help them?

The main issue that Jeff and Kim faced was that when they disagreed on something it would always result in a loud blow-out fight. They could be very affectionate with each other one minute and swearing and yelling at each other the next. They were both extremely perplexed as to why this occurred and they didn't realize it themselves. Jeff and Kim were obviously very popular and successful irrespective of each other. Prior to their relationships both of them were happy go lucky individuals, both were athletic in high school and hung around with the in crowd. They each had supportive families and were financially secure. Both were upstanding, law abiding citizens with good intentions for their lives. At the core of the couple's dispute was the problem that being a couple means that you have to share. You have to compromise with the other person's point of view.

Unlike some of the other couples in this book, Jeff and Kim had a secular outlook on life. Religious faith had never been very important to either of them. However, although

God did not seem to play a major role in life for either Jeff or Kim, it was still important for them and for all secular people to learn how to live a life filled with peace and love, both for themselves and towards others. With ECT, they were able to take significant steps in this direction.

If you think about it, doesn't that make perfect sense? When the great religions teach to "love thy neighbor as thyself" that is God's call to us to be kind, supportive, and compassionate to others and to ourselves regardless of our particular brand of faith. Or, as with Jeff and Kim, even if a person has no religion at all. Being human is the one thing that we all share in common, in every era and throughout all cultures worldwide. That is why ECT is so universal in its appeal and its success. The only requirement is to be a human being!

Regardless of the circumstances, or one's belief, or lack of belief, every single one of us is a child of God deserving of equal love and dignity as every other human soul ever created. The basic human condition, including our needs and even our failings, are the same for all. There are no exceptions to this universal rule.

As a therapist I would hope that my young clients indeed, all my clients, would be as optimistic and energetic as Jeff and Kim were in their everyday lives. The real problem with Jeff and Kim's relationship was that they jumped in very quickly to becoming lovers with each other. When they lived separately they yearned for each other. The attraction was so powerful that they leapt into getting an apartment and began to live as a couple. Instead of spending weekends apart from each other and missing each other they were now together each day. As I explained to the young couple they just needed to find a healthy balance of time spent with each other and apart from each other. Over the years I've found that regardless of age, sex or ethnicity, all couples have to work on having an emotionally healthy self, separate from a relationship with their partner. A good relationship exists when both individuals respect themselves but also support the process that a true partnership provides.

As a metaphor, I used two magnets with opposite energies. When two magnets are far apart they seek each other out. But when the magnets are too close they repel. This is just like couples do when they initially meet. When two people are too close together they repel. And they will wait for each other. It would be ideal to have a magnetic energy that was perfectly in balance all the time. But that is not realistic of life. As ECT tells us, all relationships are either growing toward us or moving away. These relationships evoke feelings in us such as joy, grief, fear and relief. All young couples including Kim and Jeff are excited and motivated to begin a relationship with their new partner. Why? It's a chance for joy. What is joy? Happiness and pleasure. We all want that authentic feeling and we are trained as kids to pursue it. You are told to save money in a piggy bank when you are little. Why? You will be able to buy things that you enjoy when you are older. Study hard in school. Why? You'll be able to get a job when you are older so you can buy new things. Or live a life with good resources.

Young people like to watch romance or love movies. Why? Everyone hopes to meet Prince Charming or a perfect girl. Eternal joy, however, is a myth that in most cases is broken quite quickly once couples start living together. Healthy relationships are usually the result of two adults committed to working on a relationship. The key is the word "work," which means time. It takes work and effort to see the other person's point of view. It takes time to learn the emotional, financial, spiritual and physical needs of a partner. The healthier relationships that I see are those where both partners really appreciate the benefit of having a partner and desire to work toward making their partner happy. That's what real maturity is, a recognition that yes I could live my life single and survive every day. The reader may ask what makes somebody want to work on a relationship with a partner. The answer is really no different than a job or career. Oftentimes people are motivated to find a job because they need money. They may initially be motivated by fear of being poor and having few resources. Others may be motivated by joy; they may have so much joy in what they are doing that they make a career out of it.

Relationships with a partner are usually motivated by the same authentic feelings of joy and fear. With Kim and Jeff, it was obvious that they had a great deal of joy motivating them to be together. But the real problem with both of these young people was that they were not used to working on a relationship on a day to day level on the four aspects of emotional, financial, spiritual and physical needs. In other words, because they jumped in so quickly they had more demands placed on them and they were overwhelmed and not used to it.

With ECT we came across certain things about the relationship with Kim and Jeff. They both had to change addresses and move and this costs money. They both had to pay for a wedding and this cost money. They had to spend more time with each other each day so they had to listen to each other more. They both had different views of religion, which meant compromise. They both had different needs physically so they had to learn a great deal about each other in a short amount of time. All of this was overwhelming to them and caused an excessive amount of fear.

When we examined Jeff and Kim's new life using Emotional Core Therapy we were able to see that they had started their relationship very quickly which led to each of them having excessive fear. Jeff was feeling afraid that he might abandon Kim because he couldn't deal with living with a woman so young in his life. He was afraid that he couldn't deal with all the drama and emotions. Kim was feeling equally fearful that she would not be able to handle all of the household chores that she felt obligated to do. She wasn't sure that she would be able to get a handle on it and take care of a man.

Over the course of several months we examined all of the four authentic feelings involved with Jeff and Kim. They were able to see that they would need to make minor adjustments and compromises for each of their needs, so that they could balance their life a little bit better. There was a reassuring feeling by both of them that they could work through their marital relationship to change their lives. The ECT approach was helpful with both Kim and Jeff as they were both able to recognize their individual feelings and work toward a resolution. One of the key things that they both did very well in therapy was to learn to relax and spend some time by themselves each day. This was so they could calm themselves down.

Much like learning to swim or ride a bike, learning to express one's feelings is a process. At the core of the process is externalizing our feelings versus internalizing them. In simple terms, externalizing one's feelings means to put something outside of the mind. In other words, the release of fear or a thought. Internalizing means to incorporate within oneself. There are good things to internalize-values, ethics, homework, anything learned-however, toxic fears are unhealthy for the mind and body. These negative stored feelings are not really healthy to keep in and they cause stress. Oftentimes people who store their feelings repeatedly have body function problems such as muscular tension, hands trembling, sweating, shaking and nightmares. Not only are these feelings uncomfortable they are unhealthy.

Jeff and Kim were able to work through the major relationship changes in their lives in a short period of time because they truly saw the benefit or having a partner and the joy it could bring. ECT was helpful to both of them as they were both able to recognize their individual feelings and work toward a resolution.

A person has to be fully capable of giving in a relationship to a partner. Let's look at all four aspects of one's needs in a relationship in a hypothetical case. This scenario involves a very healthy young lady who was vibrant successful and full of life. She meets someone like Jeff from our first example but in this case the young man gets in a car accident soon after they get together. He has surgery, loses his job and is in a lot of pain. The point is no one can predict the future or predict how relationships will work out in the future. This is all the more reason to focus on authentic feelings as a therapist and also for our clients. As we focus more on authentic feelings we move towards a better resolution and there are less surprises and less shock in one's life. With ECT we have an equal responsibility of listening to each other's needs. Meditation and relaxation are hallmarks of emotionally healthy people. Many successful people learn to balance their workplace and family responsibilities with ways to relax. As long as one can daydream and keep reflective one can let their mind relax. It doesn't have to be sitting in a yoga position or listening to your body. There are other ways to do it.

The real reason why Emotional Core Therapy is a game changer in the field of psychology is the ability for the client to "transfer" the invaluable techniques learned in this book to new relationships. For example, when you enter ECT therapy to deal with an overbearing boyfriend or girlfriend who overwhelms you to exhaustion, you learn some basic tools to protect yourself. You learn how to identify fear, feel the symptoms of fear, process those feelings, and work towards a meditative state. Once you learn a meditative state, it is easier to identify future feelings of fear with your boyfriend or girlfriend. You can then utilize these ECT techniques that you have learned to change your behavior so that you don't continue to experience these feelings over and over again. Also, you can then use these invaluable techniques to help with other relationship problems such as a domineering parent or a disrespectful friend.

Let's look at a hypothetical example of something like this in simple terms. A high school couple, Benny and Shauna, go out on a date every Friday night. Usually a movie, maybe a concert, whatever it is, always something fun. The only problem is, whenever Benny comes over to Shauna's house to pick her up, he has to wait, sometimes as much as an hour, because she is still in the bathroom "getting ready" for their date. Before long Benny begins to feels hurt and disrespected by his girlfriend. He also is very anxious about being late for whatever event he had planned for them. His authentic feelings of fear and grief affect Benny very negatively. He becomes agitated, experiences muscle tension, and even begins to lose hope. These symptoms have to be released somehow.

If Benny were to use ECT, he would discover that it is the "relationship" he has entered into that is causing him stress. He would be encouraged to change his behavior by discussing the issues with Shauna. They would change how they schedule their dates, with Shauna beginning her "preparation" time earlier in the evening so that she would be ready when Benny arrives for their date. This would make Benny begin to feel empowered in the relationship, and he would be able to release his authentic feelings of fear and grief in a constructive manner with his girlfriend, which in turn would help him to regain his normal, peaceful and meditative state.

Benny and Shauna were both Evangelical Christians. Therefore, as with every other issue in their lives, they turned to the Bible for answers. When Benny learned from ECT that fear and grief were truly the problems in his relationship, he decided to search the Scriptures to see what they had to say about the subject. One verse especially resonated with him: For God hath not given us the spirit of fear; but of power, and of love, and of a sound mind. (2 Timothy 1:7).

His whole life, Benny had been taught to trust and believe what he read in the Bible. The connection in this passage between the absence of fear, empowerment, and maintaining a God-given "sound mind" seemed to line up perfectly with the goals and techniques of ECT. Therefore, when ECT showed him appropriate ways to deal with his fear and to release it, Benny felt confident that he was doing so in accordance with the teachings of God's word.

This was extremely important to Benny, and he shared his thoughts about it with Shauna, who was also a very faithful person. She embraced ECT even more fully after realizing what a good fit it was with her Christian beliefs. Shauna's parents and her church had always instructed her to make sure that whatever choices she made in life were biblically sound. Benny's Evangelical upbringing was much the same, and as a couple they became increasingly comfortable with letting ECT help them to deal with their issues as they utilized it side by side with their deeply held Christian beliefs and practices.

Let's take the story a little bit further and say that now, two weeks later Benny has similar feelings of fear and grief when the coach on his baseball team shuffles Benny to last place in the batting order. The young man would be able to utilize the same ECT techniques he learned with his girlfriend to deal with his problem on the team. What we are discussing here is a "transferable" ability. Because ECT relies on authentic feelings, which are simple and easy to learn, the client has a much better chance of utilizing his "learned behavior" with future relationships and events in his life.

One of the most important dynamics of learning Emotional Core Therapy is the wisdom to know that traumatic grief and fear can happen to anyone. Whether one is a master at ECT or just an emotionally healthy person, we all have to live in the real world where loved ones get sick, we argue with parents, flunk a test, etc. For this very reason, it is important to equip yourself with psychological assistance that will help you over a lifetime, and not just once. With ECT, the client is empowered by the process as he is learning it in his long-term memory. He /she will own the technique.

Therapy can be an expensive process. It can hurt to shell out dollar after dollar every time you have a serious relationship issue – and you don't want to have to spend the rest of your adult life in a therapist's office! Why not become your own therapist? When you have learned ECT you can transfer this skill set to all of your relationships, wherever you go, whomever you are with. This is because ECT is fundamentally sound. In the example above, Benny has resolved the difficulty with his girlfriend and coach using ECT. Now Benny can use what he has learned in other fearful events. For example, learning how to scuba dive or explore caves, or overcoming his fear of snakes. Fear is fear, no matter what the relationship is that is causing Benny to feel debilitated. He can steer away from more fearful and grief stricken relationships because he can sense their danger. The more he can distance himself from debilitating feelings, the more powerful he can be in life with his relationships.

Another hypothetical example of how Emotional Core Therapy can help young couples involves a couple named Kareem and Talibah. They both had just graduated high school and now they had the entire summer in front of them to do whatever they wanted. Kareem's idea was to spend most of his time with his friends, skateboarding, riding dirt bikes and doing other "guy stuff." However, this didn't go over well with Talibah, who felt that now that they were both 18 and high school graduates, they should devote more time to each other. Neither had planned to go to college, but Talibah was going to school to be a medical assistant and she strongly believed that Kareem should get some job training too and tried to push him into doing so. Clearly, they didn't see things eye to eye.

However, one thing that the two of them most certainly had in common was their strong Muslim faith. They, along with their families were devout Muslims. This helped bring clarity to their relationship. Along with learning ECT, the couple decided to delve more deeply into their religion's teaching about the purposes of relationships between men and women. Unlike many Western views, in Islam, dating is seen primarily as a precursor to marriage. Kareem realized that as a young Muslim man who had just graduated high school, he did have to start getting more serious about his future, including the possibility of marrying Talibah.

In fact, their families gently reminded the couple that in Islam, the purpose of "dating" (a term they weren't particularly comfortable with in their culture) was to find a suitable marriage partner. Therefore, Kareem and Talibah should use this youthful season of life not just seeking "fun" activities on their own, but as a golden opportunity to prepare for the future that they could share together as a husband and wife.

Marriage is highly honoured in the Islamic religion. The Koran very explicitly states: "And among His Signs is this, that he created for you mates from among yourselves, that you may dwell in tranquility with them, and He has put love and mercy between your [hearts]..." Accordingly, both Kareem and Talibah would need to re-examine their relationship through the guidance of their religious faith and spiritual beliefs.

This new perspective on their relationship would require change. But couples therapy would reveal that Kareem was resentful of change. He was initially resistant to the idea of changing his relationship with Talibah. Before when they were in high school, they basically only went out together on dates on weekends and Kareem was fine with keeping things that way. But Talibah was not. As we had mentioned previously, nobody can predict the future. If they were going to save their relationship, they would have to work towards making Talibah happy. After all, it wasn't fair for only one of them to be happy, nor would their relationship be able to survive that way and lead to marriage. This meant that Kareem would have to make changes to his plans for the summer. In some manner Kareem would have to "grieve" the loss of an unlimited amount of hanging out with his guy friends and just taking it easy.

For Talibah's part, she wanted to stay with Kareem if he became a full partner in the relationship. Now that she was becoming more mature, Talibah had grown more confident in herself and her life. She had decided that if he didn't wake up and spend more time with her, she was going to leave him. Fortunately for both of them, the fear of breaking up was a motivating factor. That was in reality something that neither of them wanted.

Using ECT, Kareem and Talibah's therapist would make a list each week of the things that Talibah wanted to do and Kareem would be encouraged to work hard towards many of these things. It was not the post-graduation life he had envisioned. He had to grieve that loss. He had to process that and recognize that he had to alter certain circumstances of his life that involved reconnecting with his girlfriend.

Initially he had a lot of fear about this, i.e., spending more time with Talibah. For a long time, he had avoided her during work but once he had lived with that fear he would then be able to work toward overcoming it on a daily basis. This process might take several months, but eventually they should begin to experience a stronger, more intimate relationship that was no longer teetering on the brink of disaster.

One of the many positive aspects of Emotional Core Therapy is the ability to simplify "psychological help" so that a large sector of the population can benefit from it and use it in their daily life. Earlier in the book we discussed the prevalence of mental health problems. Inappropriate behaviors or inadequate self-soothing techniques cause many of these problems. ECT is a learned process. It relies on using your logic to learn a sequence of steps. ECT also requires you to monitor your body on a daily basis. Most Kindergartens in the United States and around the world follow similar routines. For example, learning the alphabet and following school rules. Most religions also require learning similar training. For example, reciting prayers and following rituals. There is a track record of early intervention in our educational system. So I am optimistic of ECT helping our youth. The key is making mental health a priority.

In closing, let's return to the analogy of the rudderless rowboat one more time, to see what it is that slows a person down in life. Too much water in the rowboat will slow or stop the power. Water inside the rowboat for months and years will make even a "Mercedes" rowboat travel like a paddleboat. We can see what drains the passion out of a strong person's will. It is toxic relationships that cause one to have debilitating feelings of grief and fear for long periods of time. Remember, we can all get "stuck" in hard to deal with relationships from time to time. The key, however, is to diligently apply all that you have learned about Emotional Core Therapy and keep working to find a resolution. Be determined to make whatever changes are necessary to your self-soothing techniques to try and stay calm.

List Five Ways A Couple Can Relax Together

A) GOING ON A PICNIC

B) TAKING A LONG BIKE RIDE ON A NATURE TRAIL

1.

2.

3.

4.

5.

Notes:

List Five Ways Your Partner Can Meet Your Emotional, Financial, Spiritual, and Physical Needs.

    1)

    2)

    3)

    4)

    5)

List Five Ways Your Partner Can Honor Your Four Authentic Feelings of Joy, Grief, Fear, and Relief.

1)

2)

3)

4)

5)

ECT Flow Chart

Relationships;
self, other people, places, things

⬇

Needs;
emotional, financial, spiritual, physical

⬇

Five Senses;
seeing, touching, smelling, tasting, hearing

⬇

Four Authentic Feelings;
joy, grief, fear, relief

⬇

Effects;
brain/central nervous system

⬇

Uncomfortable Symptoms;
muscle tightness, fatigue, etc.

⬇

Releasing Process;
learn to discharge toxic feelings

⬇

Balancing Your Equilibrium;
practice various daily meditative techniques

CHAPTER SIX
Using ECT to Combat Serious Stressful Situations

Emotional Core Therapy is a form of "self-care" that can help you deal with and overcome life's problems, including severely stressful situations such as dealing with the death of a loved one and overcoming addictions. The goal of this chapter is to tie together everything that you have learned so far in this book, along with some new steps that will provide you with the maximum benefits that Emotional Core Therapy has to offer.

Be patient with the process. It takes time, energy, and resources to learn about the world around you as you continue to grow and develop from an adolescent to an older teenager to a young adult. A good deal of training and education is required to truly understand how best to interact with others. That only makes sense of course. Think about the training involved to be a mechanic or hairstylist. Both take at least a year to become fully licensed. Why? There are lots of important steps to learn to help fix car engines or to give someone's hair a makeover. Fortunately, going to a local mechanic or hair stylist is easy (even though paying for it might not be so easy!). That means that most people will never need to learn the fundamentals of these important trades for themselves.

But it's very different when we're talking about human emotions. The four authentic feelings happen to all of us throughout the day whether we like it or not. The vast majority of us get a little sad or fearful on a weekly basis. At least once a year, a quarter of the population will suffer debilitating feelings of fear and grief. Is it better to ignore training on emotions and run to the nearest therapist's office every time we are troubled emotionally? I think not. An ounce of prevention is worth a pound of cure. That is what this chapter is all about. We are now going to take all that we have learned about ECT so far and take it one step further. Actually, three steps. As you will see in the flow chart at the end of the chapter, altogether there are eight basic steps to Emotional Core Therapy, and they will help you to be fully engaged in the world around you throughout your life.

Back in that early part of the book we had discussed how ECT can help in the often mentally intense sport of golf. One of the concepts I help golfers understand is that each shot is a separate relationship. Therefore, it is important to process your authentic feelings after each shot and remain in a peaceful state before you focus on your next shot. Let's take a look at this for a professional player who is playing a typical hole on a course. He will hit his drive out into the fairway. That is one shot and one relationship. Whatever experience he feels on this shot, he needs to process those feelings. In this case, he is happy with his shot so he has moments of joy. He experiences joy and releases those feelings by looking at the trees and water around him. He gets relaxed again and then prepares for his next shot in the fairway. This time he hits a poor shot into the heavy grass around the green, called the "rough". Our golfer is sad for a few minutes, but learns to release the feelings properly by processing his thoughts with his caddie. He then prepares for his next shot, which is called a chip. His ball lies deep down in the grass so he has some excess fear in his mind prior to the shot. He appropriately pays attention to his feelings of fear and changes his routine to accommodate the tough "lie or slope" of the grass. He then plays the shot and hits a nice shot hear the hole. He is quite "relieved" as he now has an easy putt to get his par and do well on the hole. His relief comes from ending a fearful event or relationship.

In my experience, golfers are some of the most stable professional athletes out there. Why? Golf requires not only power but finesse and a soft touch. The game also is filled with human emotions of fear and grief every round. You cannot take drugs or be unstable and be a high performing golfer for a prolonged period of time.

Whether it is on the golf course, or in any other aspect of life, ECT is about gaining the power and independence to choose a healthy lifestyle. It is a viable solution to fighting debilitating feelings of fear and loss because of its exacting nature. All stress comes from entering and leaving relationships. The root cause of stress is moving towards relationships that we like or dislike. One of the key advanced features of ECT is learning how to manage the relationship demands of others. Most relationships require us to meet demands. To keep things simple, we can categorize these into four areas: emotional, financial, spiritual, and physical. Using our five senses (hearing, touching, seeing, tasting, and smelling) we feel one of four ways: joyful, sad, fearful, or relieved. These four feelings can cause our mind and body various levels of discomfort. We have to release these foreign feelings to reach our normal state of relaxation/comfort. Relaxation and comfort need to be reached on a daily basis so we can continually identity foreign feelings (joy, grief, fear, and relief) and deal with them appropriately.

A therapist often acts like a parent figure to his clients. As we said earlier in the book, Mom and Dad always remind their children to dress warmly during the winter for a very good reason. Protection. It is their job to engrain in your mind and your habits the importance of physically protecting yourself to stay healthy and away from harm (such as coming down with pneumonia or getting frostbite). It's very similar to the way in which a therapist wants to help you to maintain your mental health. Of course, you can't go through life with a therapist sitting by your side, which is why Emotional Core Therapy is all about empowering yourself to understand your own emotions and how best to process them. Whether you like it or not, you will suffer fear and loss in your life. In fact, most of us will have at least some minor irritation on a daily or weekly basis. I am not a pessimistic person at all, but as a realist I know that your generation is facing some serious global economic problems that have evolved over the past few years. Many people have suffered greatly from traumatic states of fear and grief because of this and other major headaches, but it is all part of the reality of the adult world that you are quickly entering.

Just like everybody else, those who know and practice ECT will still have problems. But they will have a method for dealing with their problems that makes our often-difficult world seem that much more enjoyable. There is a bright side of life that goes beyond our difficulties, and those who know ECT find it easier to get there. One of the many positive aspects of Emotional Core Therapy is the ability to simplify "psychological help" so that virtually anyone can learn the techniques. Look at the alternative. Inappropriate behaviors or inadequate self-soothing techniques cause people all kinds of stress and heartache.

Of course, ECT is a learned process. It relies on using your logic to learn a sequence of steps. ECT also requires you to monitor your body on a daily basis. The training is based on large part on repetition. Practice makes perfect. Most Kindergartens in the United States and around the world follow similar routines. For example, learning the alphabet and following school rules. Most religions also employ similar training. For example, reciting prayers and following rituals. These are things that remain with you for life – and ECT can become an engrained (permanent) part of your life too.

My goal is for you to master the ECT process by the time you finish reading this book. To help you out even more I would like to point out that the eight-step ECT flowchart is easier to master than meets the eye. Why? The first three steps, whether we like them or not, are constant features of everybody's life on a daily basis. The first three steps are:

1) Understanding the impact that relationships have on our mind and body.
2) Understanding the needs (emotional, financial, spiritual, and physical) of people and things that we have a relationship with.
3) Having our five senses (hearing, touching, tasting, smelling, and seeing) prompt us to experience one of the four authentic feelings.

Let's look at an example to prove our point. We hear an ambulance race past us down the street with loud sirens blaring. Whether we like it or not we have entered into a relationship that causes us to use our sense of hearing to move out of the way (moving out of the way is a physical need being required of us). When it comes to our visual sense, the sight of a person that we like could bring us to experience the authentic feeling of joy, and conversely touching an oven door that is hot makes us experience fear, so that we literally move away from it. For most of us, such basic tenets of ECT will not be hard to grasp. The real challenge in learning ECT is to identify which authentic feeling is being aroused by your senses. In the case of the ambulance, it is "fear".

The next key learning technique is to monitor your body (messages are constantly being sent to your central nervous system almost unconsciously) and muscular skeletal system for adverse reactions and debilitating symptoms. What kinds of physical reactions are we talking about? It could be things such as goose bumps, chills, sweating, blushing, muscles tensing up, teeth grinding, etc. There are all kinds of physical reactions that your central nervous system is "hard wired" to respond with when various stimuli come to your brain through your five senses.

This is common to all human beings of all ages and from every culture currently or previously on the face of the Earth. Increased heart rate and breathing when a person is scared, for example, comes from the "fight or flight" instinct that kept our distant ancestors alive when they lived in very hostile environments with large predatory animals that constantly threatened them. A rush of adrenaline accompanied by these other physical reactions would give them the extra edge that they needed to either defeat or to flee potential adversaries, either animal or human. Today, our circumstances usually aren't that severe, but the basic concepts and, perhaps more importantly our bodies are pretty much the same. Therefore, when you get really nervous and your heart is racing when you have to get up and read an essay in front of the whole class, you can thank your ancient ancestors for those sweaty palms and tense shoulders!

Fortunately, one of the really cool things about Emotional Core Therapy is that it works *with* your senses and your central nervous system rather than against them. ECT doesn't deny that you will have negative energy throughout your life, or try to wish it away, but instead it teaches you to learn how to release it.

We had also mentioned the importance of learning to meet the various demands of people we are in relationships with. Let's briefly look at each of these:

Emotional: Just as you want to be emotionally healthy (which is what ECT is all about) your actions and behaviors will affect the emotional needs of those around you. For example, your parents want to feel secure that you are safe and happy. You can meet this emotional need that they have by showing them that you are maturing at a good pace and becoming a responsible young person. This will very much help to put their mind at ease.

Financial: Even teenagers have an impact on the financial needs of others, though perhaps not as much as adults. Sure, you probably don't have a family to support, but you are at the age where what you do impacts the financial needs of others. For example, can you help your family with college costs by working part-time? Also, by studying hard you can earn scholarship money that can also help ease the financial demands on your parents.

Spiritual: When you think about it, spirituality is ageless. You could be 15 or 95, when it comes to eternal spiritual things those numbers don't mean very much. We are all the same. Human beings experience all kinds of spiritual states. You may have a friend, for example, who is at a very low point in his life. He can't see beyond the misery of his current circumstances. You can lift him out of the spiritual doldrums just by being a good listener. In other words, just by being there for him as a good friend you are helping to fulfill his spiritual needs. Spiritual often has a religious connotation and helps people to feel relaxed, hopeful and positive about the future. Yet we should also realize that there are other ways to be spiritual, too.

Physical: Oftentimes people mistake "physical" for "sexual," and although that can be a part of it, meeting the physical needs of others covers much more than just intimacy. It can also mean, for example, helping a friend who is trying to get into shape. Or it might mean keeping your little sister safe when she is outside playing by keeping a close eye on her. There are all kinds of ways that you can help with the physical needs of the people in your life.

Emotional Core Therapy teaches us that a diligent effort to maintain peace and relaxation is needed to remind the body of its normal state of comfort. For nearly all of us, it will take a few months at the very least to master these techniques.

This only makes sense, because we are retraining our mind and body, which takes time and effort. Nothing comes easy, but the reward of a healthy and balanced lifestyle is well worth the effort.

Make no mistake about it, you don't want to underestimate the time and work involved in understanding and utilizing Emotional Core Therapy. It sometimes takes between two and eight months to get full relief from debilitating feelings of grief and fear. Over the years I have seen many people who desire a quick fix for emotional issues that have no easy cure. That's not how it normally works. In some cases, there may be no complete solution in the short-term, only partial remedies. This is just as true for adults as it is for teenagers. For example, if a man who is supporting a large family works at a job where he absolutely hates his tyrant of a boss, this would cause him a good deal of anxiety and stress. However, leaving that situation, especially in today's terrible employment environment, probably would not be practical for this man. He could not economically afford it, so he would need to use ECT to come up with at least some partial relief.

You will likely find situations like that in your own life too, not necessarily involving a job, but other things that you have very little control over. Maybe your parents decide to move the family to another part of the country. You're under eighteen so you have no choice but to go along with the move even if you're totally opposed to it. As we all know, that's just the way life is sometimes. Still, ECT will help you to maintain your peace of mind and realize that even things that seem like the biggest problems in the world are manageable when you learn, memorize and practice the right techniques.

The following are hypothetical yet realistic examples of how solving problems can take an extended period of time before seeing any improvement. The first case involves a high school junior girl named Devani. One day, Devani suddenly finds that she has to move far away from where she grew up after her dad gets a job transfer to another state. This young lady had built loving and trusting relationships with friends since birth and now she wouldn't be able to see them any longer. This type of grief or loss can take months and maybe a year or so to process and cathartically release the pain. It would be completely unrealistic to just expect her feelings to somehow magically change overnight.

Devani was Hindu and her faith taught her that suffering, including mental anguish, was a result of karma. However, her Hindu faith also taught Devani the principle of detachment, which involves not becoming overwhelmed by life's problems. This is, she was pleased to learn, also one of the goals of ECT. Specific tools for achieving detachment include meditation and yoga, which again were a perfect fit with ECT and therefore more of a reason for Devani to fully embrace them. These tools teach the understanding and control of one's mind, and seeing beyond one's mind to God.

In fact, Hinduism taught Devani that the focus of one's life should be on God. When priority is given to this inner journey, with less focus on the world, processing one's pain, as ECT equips you to do, becomes a spiritual as well as a psychological endeavor, which Devani found quite appealing, not to mention helpful.

Another example would be a high school sophomore boy, Kyle, whose father is dying of cancer. In all likelihood Kyle would face fear and grief for a year or two on a daily basis. His suddenly secure world is changing for the worse, and it must feel like everything is crumbling around him. This type of tragic situation of course takes a good deal of time and work to understand and cope with to resolve.

Unlike many people facing the grief of losing a loved one, Kyle did not have religious faith to help him through the process. Though never hostile to religion or the idea of God, spirituality had just never been an important part of life for Kyle. Nonetheless, with his secular outlook on life, he was able to use ECT to help him through this difficult transition in his life. He learned more about his own life, and his outlook on the things that he wanted to do and to achieve while he himself was still living. It also gave him a greater appreciation for the love and togetherness that he found with close family and friends.

While a religious young person might lean on his or her faith during a tough life experience such as Kyle's, even without strong religious or spiritual beliefs Kyle was able to incorporate ECT into his daily life in ways that made him more emotionally stable and capable of withstanding the heart rending feelings he sometimes found himself having to endure.

Moreover, friends of Kyle who themselves were religious kept him in their prayers and told him so. Even though he did not completely understand or concur with their spiritual activities, he genuinely appreciated the gesture and it made him realize how much other people, including his ECT therapist, cared about him and very much wanted to help him with his healing.

A third situation would be a high school freshman girl, Lexi, who gets overly ambitious and takes too many hard classes for her first year in high school. The demands she faces cause excess fear from September to June of her school year. Her problem is deep, and not likely to quickly disappear.

Lexi found ECT to be extremely helpful with her fears. She also liked the way that it fit in so well with her lifelong Catholic faith. Simplicity when it comes to calming the mind is one of the hallmarks of the Catholic faith. With Lexi's devotion to the Blessed Mother, she found that letting her mind wander while looking at a statue of the Virgin Mary that her late grandmother had given to her when she was a little girl helped her tremendously.

This form of meditation brought Lexi's mind back to a simpler time in her life, when school was pleasant for her instead of a burden. It helped the teen to realize that her problems were not with classes, they were with her own perspective on things, which was mostly based upon fear. Meditating on thoughts of her beloved grandmother, and of the Blessed Mother, put Lexi in a much more peaceful frame of mind, just as ECT was teaching her how to do. This didn't solve all of her problems, but it certainly made them much more manageable.

All three of these examples are very typical of the kinds of things that can and do happen to many high school adolescents. There is no cure for these emotional issues but having a good support system in place is an important piece of the puzzle. In fact, it is indispensable. A good support system would help each one of these emotionally bothered kids to identify and process their feelings. Ultimately, this would help to bring joy into their lives.

I would like to also like to share with you in this chapter the case of Rebecca. Rebecca saw me for mental health and substance abuse issues for a period of seven months. Rebecca told me her troubles began several years ago when she was a senior in high school. During Rebecca's intake evaluation, we discovered a strained relationship with her father and losing contact with some close friends as they made the transition into college and the working field. Rebecca and I worked hard in therapy to deal with her addiction issues with alcohol, marijuana and a junk food diet.

I treated Rebecca using my Emotional Core Therapy flow chart. A key part of our treatment was educating Rebecca on the toxic feelings associated with addictions that can adversely affect your life. We utilized the Internet to research the dangers associated with alcohol, marijuana and a junk food diet. An important point to remember with those suffering addictions is to educate them on the many ways that toxic addictions can hurt you.

Another way that ECT is a unique process is the aspect of focusing on "ever changing needs" that can cause one stress. For Rebecca, she needed time and support to comprehend the dangerous relationship needs she was involved in on a daily basis. I often ask my clients, "What's this relationship you are choosing doing for you? Are you fully informed about the dangers? This gives the client the power to make better decisions going forward.

Another key point to focus on relating to Rebecca's case was the occurrence of regression during the treatment process. Why? Addictions can be very powerful. It is rare that I see an individual recover in a short span from their addictions when they are experiencing a great deal of emotional and physical pain. Rebecca was no different. She had periods of growth but also some setbacks.

The goal of Emotional Core Therapy is to help clients identify the toxics feelings they experience in their daily life when they enter into an addictive relationship. This is not an overnight process. Oftentimes the treatment plan takes place over the course of weeks or several months. The reason that therapy can take extended periods of time is that addictions are learned behaviors that are acquired over the course of several months, even years. The human mind takes time to learn new behaviors both negative and positive. It can take several weeks or months to learn ECT, aside from relieving the suffering associated with addictions.

I shared with Rebecca the Greek fable of the young boy Icarus. Icarus was warned by his father to not travel too close to the sun with his wings made up of clay, wax and feathers. Icarus ignored the warning of his father and flew near the hot sun. His wings melted and he fell to the earth and perished. Individuals can seek temporary power, such like Icarus, from their addictions in order to escape the sufferings associated with negative feelings. ECT shows you how to gain genuine and long lasting power. This is done through having healthy relationships with yourself and others that bring the authentic feeling of joy.

To accomplish the treatment objective of finding real joy, Rebecca and I worked together to create a list of 10 relationships that would bring authentic joy into her life. Each week Rebecca and I worked together using ECT to establish the relationships on her treatment plan. Rebecca was close with her mother, Cheryl. Rebecca, Cheryl and I worked together to implement a positive and supportive treatment plan to provide motivation for Rebecca to use ECT to change her behaviors. The incentive in Rebecca's treatment plan was for Cheryl to pay for gas and insurance for Rebecca's vehicle.

Rebecca's father also played a role in the treatment process. The father would often use negative reinforcement and the possibility of negative consequences to influence a change in Rebecca's behavior. We worked with the father to help him see the negative effects that his communication methods had on Rebecca. The father's poor communication skills drove him away from Rebecca. They also hindered Rebecca's desire to make a change in her life by getting treatment. In therapy Rebecca was able to realize that she was internalizing her feelings of fear from her father, and turning to substances for temporary relief.

Over time Rebecca was able to gain power over her addictive behavior. She was becoming more aware that she was responsible for entering into her addictive relationships. (Step one of the ECT Flowchart). We looked at how entering relationships with ourselves, others people, places and things can cause stress in our life. Rebecca worked on changing her relationship with herself, her parents, her social network, and her addictions, to create a more emotionally balanced lifestyle.

The substances that Rebecca used to feed her addiction, such as alcohol, marijuana, and junk food adversely affected her body and mind. These substances have a physical makeup which cause harm to those like Rebecca, who digest or inhale it into their system. (Step two of ECT Flowchart)

Rebecca was able to realize that her body's ability to receive the same "high" from these substances was diminishing over time. Rebecca even spent four days in a treatment hospital to manage the physical effects associated with withdrawal from alcohol. Her five senses were being altered by her relationship with her addictions. (Step three of ECT Flowchart)

Using ECT, Rebecca and I were able to identify her authentic feeling of fear and grief relating to the addiction of the substances. Some of her emotional duress was caused by the expensive treatment and the physical pain that she endured. (step four of the ECT Flowchart)

Rebecca became aware of these feelings and they became registered in her brain. (This is step five of the ECT Flowchart). Step five is a step that comes naturally to most people.

Being more aware of her feelings helped Rebecca gain power over her addictions and negative behavior. This allowed her to move forward with the treatment of ECT. Rebecca and I would review the flowchart weekly. Over time she gained a firm command of the ECT process. Having the flowchart at her hands was a safety net for Rebecca. She was able to identify her uncomfortable physical symptoms which included lack of sleep, irritability, stomach pain, digestive problems, and weight gain. She also identified crippling feelings of fear and grief. (Step six of the ECT Flowchart.)

Once we were able to eliminate the intake of negative substances into her body Rebecca began to feel better. The physical discomfort she had identified was slowly decreasing. Rebecca also began to release the toxic feelings of grief and fear from her addictions. (Step seven of the ECT Flowchart)

Rebecca was to maintain peace and balance in her daily life. We worked together to emphasize quiet time for reflection and meditation. She found ways to let her mind wander and freely float from thought to thought. When her life began to slow down for Rebecca she began to make better decisions for herself. (Step eight of the ECT Flowchart)

Meditation is a great way to care and respect your mind and body. I like to have clients such as Rebecca look back to a time in their life where they were most peaceful. Rebecca remembered when she was 12 years old when she would go to the lake with her family. She loved swimming and camping. We incorporated the same peace and balance that she experienced when she was 12, into her daily life as a young adult. Rebecca incorporated her love of nature by going on frequent walks with her dog, and jogging in the local parks as a way to relax. By taking this time for herself during her day she had greater success examining all of the relationships in her life.

Rebecca and her family were members of the Southern Baptist Church. This facet of her life helped her deal with the challenges of her addiction in a number of ways. First, the teachings of her religion stressed prohibitions against using alcohol and other drugs. Knowing that there was a moral issue involved, as well as physical and psychological, gave Rebecca added incentive to make the important changes that she knew she needed to make in her life. These teachings made it clear to Rebecca that it was God's will for her to overcome her addictions. Moreover, though the church taught that abusing alcohol and drugs was sinful, it also taught that God was forgiving. He understands human weaknesses and failings, and that is why the key to all Baptist theology is that

Christ died so that people could be forgiven of every possible sin, and, just as importantly, He will strengthen them to resist the temptation to continue in their sinful lifestyle.

When it came to meditation, Rebecca's Baptist upbringing almost instinctively led her to turn to the Bible, which is front and center in the church's teachings. She was delighted to recall that the first psalm in the Book of Psalms, in describing a righteous man, states: *his delight is in the law of the Lord, and on his law he meditates day and night.*

Another Bible verse that brought peace into Rebecca's life also came from the Psalms: *The Lord is close to the brokenhearted and saves those who are crushed in spirit.* In her deepest, darkest moments, she often felt that these words were spoken by God specifically for her benefit. This made perfect sense to Rebecca, because her church taught her that the Lord did indeed reach out and speak directly to His people, both as a community of faith and as individual believers, through His Word.

For Rebecca, such scriptures meant that delving into God's word, and reading it in a spiritual way was the best method of meditation, and would bring her closer to God. She spoke to her pastor, and he pointed her to numerous other biblical passages that spoke of the power of meditation, and showed her how prayerfully reflecting on the Bible and its message of redemption and healing could help lead to her recovery.

Initially, Rebecca rated her level of emotional pain at a nine on a one to ten scale. Using ECT, Rebecca was able to reduce her emotional and physical suffering down to a level of two for most of her day. Each person is different in their level of self-awareness. Rebecca had a sense of accomplishment that she had grown through examining and changing her relationships.

Another case of a successful resolution to an addiction problem was found in the case of Cheng. Cheng lived with his mom, dad, and older sister and worked as an electrician during the day. When he came to me, he was clearly suffering from substance abuse and anger management issues. He was arrested for a DUI which resulted into legal and financial strain. He was required to hire an attorney and pay assigned court fines as well as lose his driving privileges. Cheng was also arrested for Assault during a bar fight only three months after his DUI arrest. He was very fearful of going to jail so he began to seek out counseling as treatment for his emotional duress. Cheng and I worked together several times a week, over a period of three months, to learn how to apply ECT as a way to deal with his emotional stress that was spiraling out of control. Cheng's heavy drinking was a result of his feelings of rejections by his father over his career choice as an electrician. Cheng's father was a successful businessman and looked down upon a position in the skilled trades.

Cheng's father spent his money lavishly on Cheng's mother and sister. Over time Cheng perceived himself as the black sheep of the family as he was often excluded from family functions. Cheng did not dare show his anger towards his father. He found himself acting out in fist fights with strangers over trivial matters. When he went to court for the events related to his substance abuse, the judge expressed his desire for an immediate change in Cheng's lifestyle or face the consequence of time in jail. In our treatment sessions, Cheng and I were able to identify the anger and violent acts he displayed was related to his father. This unresolved anger towards his father was the underlying cause for Cheng's emotional pain. We began to process feelings of grief during therapy by utilizing several of the ECT techniques discussed in this book to release the toxic feelings in Cheng's life.

One method that we used in therapy which was not discussed in previous chapters is the technique of using psychodrama. Psychodrama is an action method of therapy which uses dramatization and role playing to gain insight into the individual's behavior. By acting out his feeling of rejection by his father out in a psychodrama scene, Cheng was finally able to make sense of his emotional pain. He suffered from a combination of mental health and substance abuse issues. ECT helped treat both emotional problems.

The son of Chinese immigrants, Cheng had been brought up learning (mostly from his mother) about Taoism, a religious and philosophical system developed in ancient China. As he grew older, and the more he read about Taoist beliefs and practices, Cheng became intrigued by it. He realized that this ageless wisdom could help bring a strong measure of peace and balance into his often tumultuous life.

Now, as Cheng started using ECT, he began relying on Taoist principles even more as he learned healthy ways to release his emotions. For example, key teachings of Taoism include freeing oneself from selfishness and desire, and appreciating simplicity. These ideals helped Cheng to relax and let his mind enter a meditative state. He no longer felt so trapped by his circumstances, which, along with ECT helped him to start dealing with his anger issues in healthier ways.

As Cheng continued to learn more about Taoism, especially by faithfully reading one of its most sacred texts, the "I Ching," he embraced the philosophy whole-heartedly. It teaches that the universe works harmoniously according to its own ways. Therefore, when a person asserts their will in ways that are contrary to this harmony, it causes all kinds of personal disruptions and problems. Cheng could really identify with this, because he had been experiencing so much turmoil in his own life.

To restore the natural balance that we all want in life, Cheng used the Taoist principle of "non-action." The underlying idea is that many times it is not necessary for people to deliberately take any specific actions at all, or to follow a set plan. It reasserts the Taoist belief that the universe will ultimately restore perfect harmony and balance to all things, without human intervention. This does not mean literally doing nothing; rather, it is an approach to life that emphasizes spontaneity and creativity. Cheng soon discovered that this "living in the moment" kind of thinking, which is so integral to Taoism, was also an ideal fit with ECT, which teaches people how to be aware of their own emotions and to process them in ways that will lead to more peaceful relations with others and, just as importantly, with themselves.

The Taoist concept of the "Three Treasures" also aided in Cheng's recovery. They are: compassion, moderation, and humility. Put into practice alongside ECT, these Taoist principles helped to guide Cheng into a healthier lifestyle.

Emotional Core therapy was a good fit for Cheng for many other reasons, too. For example, we were able to apply the psychological techniques of ECT to all of his relationship issues. We spent some time in therapy discussing his anger and other times discussing his substance abuse issues. Using the ECT flow chart, Cheng was able to regain power over his life. Reviewing the flowchart each week was an efficient way to monitor his emotional state. Cheng was able to identify the self-defeating habits that were the root cause of his legal and financial trouble. Cheng's father was not willing to change his behaviors that were hurting him. It was going to be up to Cheng to decide what kind of relationship he wanted with his angry father. By using ECT, Cheng and I were able to identify the reality that minimized contact with his father was a healthy way to limit that cause of grief in his life.

Cheng began to spend more time outside the home as a way to create distance from his father. Cheng also kept the dialogue and conversation with his father at a minimum. This lowered Cheng's level of anger. As we mentioned in chapter four, anger is a reaction to grief. The more that Cheng was able to identify and process his grief, the quicker he was able to move towards healthier relationships. When Cheng was outside the home he began to talk with the neighbors and began to connect with them on an improved level for support and friendship. Cheng also began to take walks into town and visit more places. He enjoyed his tiny new discoveries and felt proud of himself for trying something new and different. I often tell my clients when one door closes another window opens. It is my way of showing optimism and hope to people that are making tough relationship choices along with changes in their lives.

To help the reader examine the emotional growth of Cheng in therapy I will again use the ECT Flowchart. By using the ECT Flowchart the reader can see the learning process that entails working in therapy. Nothing is easy in life that is worthwhile. As the Buddhist say, "Through suffering comes enlightenment." Sometimes working on an individual step of ECT can take weeks or months, depending on the severity of the problem. As we mentioned previously, there are five or six main components of the ECT Flowchart that require work and insight into how to learn. Several of the steps happen to most of us very quickly. Another important point to remember is that some people have knowledge and ability in one or two steps and need help on certain other steps. People have to assess their own ability and knowledge in and open and honest fashion. Therapy can help in that process.

Getting back to Cheng's case, we examined that Cheng's toxic relationship with his dad was causing his anger. (Step one of the ECT Flowchart was understanding he had entered into a new relationship.)

The reason this was hard for Cheng was that the father had emotional and financial needs that Cheng was not able to meet. Cheng's father would leave him out of family functions or belittle him in front of family and friends. (Step two of the ECT Flowchart was understanding that new relationships bring new needs from others.)

Cheng would sense his father's ill will towards him through his senses. He would see and hear complaints periodically throughout the week. (Step three of the ECT Flowchart was understanding how we examine stress through our senses.)

This brought up feelings of fear and anger/grief with Cheng. (Step Four of the ECT Flowchart was understanding how we authentically feel when stress hits us.)

A constant message of fear and grief was sent to Cheng's brain. (Step five of the ECT Flowchart tells us what each feeling signals to our brain.)

Cheng felt uptight, stressed out, and agitated around his father. (Step Six of the ECT Flowchart tells us what bodily symptoms occur when we feel stress.)

Cheng was unable to show his feelings towards his father as he felt ashamed and weak. He had his own ways of dealing with this at home. Sometimes he would squeeze his stress ball. Sometimes he would punch a punching bag. Sometimes he would go out and yell and scream in the backyard. These were all ways that Cheng used to "externalize" his feelings. In our counseling sessions we used some common psychological techniques mentioned earlier in the book to release stress like journaling and assertiveness training. This step is crucial to understanding the ECT process. Why? We are constantly cathartically releasing stress throughout the day. Emotionally healthy people do this to cleanse their soul. (Step Seven of the ECT Flowchart is the releasing process. Learning to discharge feelings.)

Over time Cheng learned to find quiet time for himself during the day to meditate and relax. This allowed him to regain a sense of himself. We revisited earlier times in his life when he relaxed such as bowling. When Cheng bowled he was able to let his mind wander and daydream. His thoughts would be free floating and he became relaxed. It is important to note others may find bowling stressful. That is why you have to research each individual's past to see what suits them best. Cheng would use bowling along with other meditative exercises to self soothe himself. (Step Eight of the ECT Flowchart is to balance your equilibrium.)

It is important to note we would do this ECT process for some of Cheng's other relationship problems like alcohol and violence towards others. As you can see from reading the case of Cheng and others in this book it takes time and energy to work through tough emotional states. This is all the more reason to be supportive of anyone who is going through a lifestyle change.

Throughout our counseling sessions I would have Cheng rate his level of emotional pain. As we made inroads into Duane's relationship stressors his level of pain dropped considerably. Having clients rate themselves is a great way to monitor their growth in therapy. It is rare I see someone go straight to recovery from a nine or ten to a one. Usually there is some back and forth movement. That is all the more reason to be kind to yourself while you are learning to understand emotions.

It is also very important, actually it is absolutely essential, to meditate daily. Don't confuse this with some kind of chanting or religious ritual (unless that is what works for you). By meditation, I am referring more broadly to allowing your mind to daydream, wander and reflect. Not only is this practice very beneficial for your mental health, but it also allows you to cathartically release pent up feelings. Throughout this book we have given lots of examples of things that people can do that can help them meditate such as praying, yoga, soaking in a jacuzzi, taking a walk, etc. The goal with all of this is to learn to monitor, identify and release the four authentic feelings, which are temporary states of being. The peace and stability that this can bring to your life is immeasurable.

One of the best ways to banish depression from your thinking is to concentrate and spend time on the things that bring you joy. A therapist using ECT will often ask his client to search their memories for specific times when they were happy. What were they doing? What did it involve? What do they remember about it that they liked so much? The list for each person might look very different. For example, this could be Devani's list:

1. Spending an afternoon at the spa

2. Riding her bike

3. Listening to music in her bedroom

4. Painting with watercolors

5. Shopping for new clothes

6. Writing poetry

7. Walking the dog

8. Looking at old pictures in a photo album

9. Baking cookies and other stuff with her mom

10. Watching game shows on TV

Kyle's list, on the other hand, could include these top ten things that bring him joy:

1. Snowboarding

2. Playing chess

3. Swimming

4. Building model airplanes

5. Lifting weights

6. Practicing guitar

7. Playing video games

8. Going to church on Sunday mornings

9. Reading comic books

10. Watching sports on TV

Lexi would have her own list. Since we are all individuals, she may or may not share some of the same or similar items on her list, which only makes sense since we are all human yet each one of us is unique.

This would be the list of the top ten things that bring Lexi joy:

1. Taking a bubble bath

2. Playing Frisbee with her dog

3. Shopping

4. Working out in front of an aerobics video on TV

5. Chatting on the phone about boys with her friends

6. Visiting with her grandparents

7. Jogging

8. Reading old diary entries from when she was younger

9. Playing basketball with her little brother

10. Reading celebrity magazines

What about your list? No matter how many down times we might have in life, never forget about all of those things that bring you happiness. My hope is that what you have learned in this book will make you realize just how much power you have to control your own life and your own destiny. You are only young once and you should enjoy the ride for all it's worth.

Once you have read this book from cover to cover, you can then assess how much knowledge you have attained learning the ECT process. If you can only recall six of the eight steps, for example, you can then focus on learning the remaining two steps, without having to reread the whole book. The important thing is to know that, like life itself, ECT is an ongoing process. This book will always be there for you to refer back to, but as time goes by you will find more and more that you do not need to keep reading it. That's because Emotional Core Therapy will empower you to help yourself. It shows you a healthy way of life that never runs away from being human, but instead fully embraces it.

EMOTIONAL CORE THERAPY TEST. Answers are at bottom of test. By doing this test you will allow your mind to have another way to commit the ECT process to your long term memory. If you are not sure of an answer, try and find the answer in the book. This will help you learn ECT. Also, the way to master the ECT approach is to retake the quiz by doing only the answers you incorrectly answered.

1) According to the ECT approach, the four authentic feelings that arise from relationship stress are?

A) Happiness, depression, fear, love

B) Joy, anxiety, sadness, anger

C) Joy, grief, fear, and relief

D) Joy, fear, anger, grief.

2) The predominant state of a person that has successfully learned ECT is?

A) Happiness, love, and lust

B) Assertiveness and calmness

C) Tranquility and balanced equilibrium

D) Loving and positive nature.

3) According to the ECT approach, the root cause of emotional stress is caused by?

A) Associating with angry and violent people

B) Being angry with your parents.

C) Holding onto anger in your body and Mind

D) Entering and leaving relationships that evoke one of the four true feelings.

4) According to the ECT approach, the four authentic feelings are?

A) Permanent states of being

B) Temporary states of being

C) Both permanent and temporary states of being

D) Neither permanent nor temporary states of being

5) According to the ECT approach, a healthy mind occurs when?

A) A person allows their mind time each day to meditate, daydream, and relax

B) A person holds onto feelings of grief and fear for several years

C) Learns to focus only on positive thoughts

D) Stays permanently away from negative people

6) The ECT Flowchart entails?

A) Five steps to learning to identify and process emotions

B) Six steps to identify and process emotions

C) Seven steps to identify and process emotions

D) Eight steps to identify and process emotions

7) According to ECT, relationships with ourselves or others usually involve which needs to be met?

A) Emotional, religious, physical, and financial

B) Emotional, financial, spiritual, and physical

C) Emotional, financial, spiritual, and sexual

D) Cognitive, financial, spiritual, and physical

8) The five senses needed to process emotions are

A) Seeing, touching, feeling, tasting, and listening

B) Believing, hearing, touching, tasting, and hearing

C) Hearing, touching, smelling, tasting, and seeing

D) Seeing, believing, touching, tasting, and hearing

9) When learning the ECT approach it is important to?

A). Focus on yourself and learn the ECT process by meditating three hours a day.

B). Focus on rewards and consequences to learn the ECT approach

C). Find a teacher to help you learn the ECT approach.

D). Be kind, supportive, and reward yourself to help learn the ECT approach

10) In order for ECT to be of real value, the process needs to be?

A) Available nearby so you can access the ECT Flowchart

B) Taught in most school aged classrooms

C) Taught as part of marital therapy

D) Learned and committed to one's long term memory through repetition

11) ECT emphasizes that stress can come to us hourly and daily. Therefore, we need to release these emotions hourly and daily as a learned habit like brushing your teeth. The "cleansing of the soul" is called?

A) Catharsis

B) Internalization

C) Suppression of emotions

D) Reflection

12) Feelings of sadness or unhappiness. Crying spells. Loss of interest or pleasure in normal activities. Fatigue, tiredness, and loss of energy. These are all symptoms of?

A) Anxiety

B) Anger

C) Depression

D) Addiction

13) According to ECT, symptoms of anxiety include which of the following?

A) Having an increased heart rate, breathing rapidly, sweating, and trembling

B) Being angry throughout the day

C) Being assertive with your angry father

D) Losing hope and feeling suicidal

14) Some symptoms of anger are the following?

A) Feeling hopeless and not wanting to be with friends

B) Feeling tired all the time and not being able to sleep

C) Feeling hot, flushed and agitated. Tension in shoulders and neck

D) Not wanting to deal with conflict at home or work

15) According to ECT, anger is a reaction to which one of the four authentic feelings?

A) Joy

B) Grief

C) Fear

D) Relief

16) A way to gauge someone's success in learning ECT is to?

A) The more you can learn and acquire the steps of the ECT Flowchart the more confident you will feel about yourself

B) Learn to stay peaceful and obtain a Zen meditation lifestyle

C) Learn to control your anger at home and work by at all times

D) Learn to only stay in relationships that bring you joy

17) Guilt happens when we hurt other human beings. The underlying authentic emotion of someone who is feeling guilty is?

A) Joy

B) Grief

C) Fear

D) Relief

18) ECT is successful when used to help couples because of which of the following?

A) ECT can help gain autonomy for both partners by having them gain peace and vitality in their lives

B) ECT can cut in half the cost of marital therapy by resolving issues quickly once and for all

C) ECT can help couples dissolve relationships with former lovers who are still in the picture

D) ECT can eliminate all negativity from a couple's life while on vacation

19) The definition of an addiction is which of the following?

A) A need for something that you can't do without on a daily basis

B) A compulsive need to make money above all other priorities in your life

C) A compulsive physiological and psychological need for a habit forming substance

D) A desire to which you cannot control and for which you need professional help

20) Individuals seek temporary emotional power through the use of any addiction. ECT helps you find genuine and long lasting power by helping you find relationships that bring which authentic feeling?

A) Joy

B) Grief

C) Fear

D) Relief

Answers. 1) C. 2) C. 3) D. 4). B. 5). A. 6). D. 7). B. 8). C. 9). D. 10). D. 11). A. 12). C. 13). A. 14). C. 15) B. 16). A. 17). B. 18). A. 19). C. 20). A.

IF YOU STILL NEED HELP LEARNING ECT DO THE FOLLOWING. MAKE A LIST BELOW OF TEN STRESSFUL EVENTS IN YOUR LIFE. JUST LIKE WE DID WITH CHENG AND REBECCA, PROCESS EACH OF THESE EVENTS USING THE EIGHT STEP ECT FLOWCHART.

1)

2)

3)

4)

5)

6)

7)

8)

9)

10)

ECT Flow Chart

Relationships;
self, other people, places, things

⇩

Needs;
emotional, financial, spiritual, physical

⇩

Five Senses;
seeing, touching, smelling, tasting, hearing

⇩

Four Authentic Feelings;
joy, grief, fear, relief

⇩

Effects;
brain/central nervous system

⇩

Uncomfortable Symptoms;
muscle tightness, fatigue, etc.

⇩

Releasing Process;
learn to discharge toxic feelings

⇩

Balancing Your Equilibrium;
practice various daily meditative techniques